The Greatest Lawyer That Ever Lived

Patrick Henry at the Bar of History

Published by Telford Publications*

Design by 875 *Design*
Illustrations by David Eccles

© George Morrow 2011

Telford Publications
P. O. Box 5904,
Williamsburg, VA, U.S.A., 23188

Tel (757) 565-7215
Fax (757) 565-7216
e-mail: telfordpublications@msn.com
www.telfordpublications.com

FIRST EDITION

**Telford Publications is named for Alexander Telford,*
a volunteer rifleman from Rockbridge County, Virginia, who
served in three Revolutionary War campaigns, in the last of which,
Yorktown, he was personally recognized by Gen. George Washington
for his extraordinary marksmanship with the long rifle.

ISBN 978-0-9831468-1-0
Printed and bound by Sheridan Press, 450 Fame Avenue, Hanover, PA

The Greatest Lawyer That Ever Lived

Patrick Henry at the Bar of History

George Morrow

WILLIAMSBURG IN CHARACTER

Patrick Henry by Thomas Sully
"Momentarily in a state of repose"

For Joan

"If a man could say nothing against a character but what he can prove, history could not be written."
SAMUEL JOHNSON

Contents

List of Illustrations

Preface

Living with Patrick Henry

In the Strange Occupations department, I respectfully submit my job as a candidate for the top spot. I make my living by being politically incorrect and insensitive, but I am not a talk show host on your AM dial. I am a Founding Father, and that is precisely what I write in the Occupation blank on my Federal tax return each year. The Internal Revenue Service hasn't called me on it yet, but I'm ready with an answer.

On any given day, I may shock and offend my listeners by justifying slavery, for example, or by convincing them that women have no place whatsoever in politics and government. I persuade my listeners to pay annual taxes to support the Christian religion only. I may declare that in order to preserve liberty every man ought to have a gun. Perhaps I'll rail about the idiocy of public education. I will be speaking in a manner that seems rather odd to most, and not just with regard to the content of my discourse, but because of the general composition and cadence of my sentences. And I will be clad in knee breeches and wearing a wig. I'm not just any Founding Father, either. I am THE Founding Father. I am Patrick Henry, Jr., Esq., of Hanover County, Virginia.

In 1995, the Programming Division at Colonial Williamsburg asked me to consider portraying Patrick Henry on a full-time basis. Initially, I declined, because I didn't really know all that much about the statesman, but also because I've always found playing The Villain to be far more theatrically rewarding.

In my extensive acting experience, I've had the most fun

when I'm booed and hissed upon entering. And who's going to boo and hiss a patriot? No, make me Benedict Arnold, or Lord Dunmore, or a British spy, or any Frenchman. But, urged to reconsider, I began learning about the man I have since endeavored "to become." I was in for a very big surprise.

Ask Americans to name some Founding Fathers, and the odds are that very few will include Henry in their honor roll. Most Americans, if they know anything at all about him, know that he once said something or other about liberty or death, but they don't know the impetus or consequences of that stirring oration. I would wager that a great many erroneously believe that Henry was a Boston man, or that he was hanged for treason, or that he was just a fellow who didn't put his money where his big yap was. These misconceptions might be due in part to the manner in which the Revolutionary period has been taught in schools for many years. Most of my own schoolmates hated History class because, after all, it's just a bunch of old facts and dates and, since it's the heaviest textbook, it's a burden to lug around. As historian David McCullough once put it, history is a bitter pill that simply has to be swallowed.

Frankly, I wasn't so enthused about the Age of Enlightenment myself – I found the Roman Empire far more exciting because of its bloodthirstiness, duplicity, and conspiracy. I somehow came to see Caligula, for example, as a real human being with desires, flaws, and an extremely warped sense of humor, like me!

By contrast, George Washington and his contemporaries weren't men – they were gods to whom we were supposed to show nothing but reverence and gratitude. Thomas Jefferson? Well, heck! He wrote the Declaration of Independence, ya gotta love him, right? It's the law!

Friends, I have seen the light. In 15 years of constant research into the 18th century in Virginia, I have come to know all these icons as men with desires, flaws and, occasionally, warped senses of humor, complete with duplicity and conspiracy. I've read their letters and journals.

I've read the newspapers and many of the books and pamphlets they read and wrote. I even know what they all looked like. Through time, I've been able to accomplish something that is often much harder for casual students of history to do – I've humanized them. For me, they are now real, not mythical beings or simply names on a page, but real men who have a lot to say to Americans in the Here and Now.

Fifteen years on, I confidently proclaim that nobody will speak to the 21st century more succinctly and eloquently than Patrick Henry, even though he died in 1799. My assignment at Colonial Williamsburg is not simply to deliver his words to the present generation in an interesting and entertaining manner; I am also to teach visitors about the 18th century in general, to impress on them the importance of the part played by the capital of colonial Virginia in a bold new experiment, and to reveal the principles that lay behind the founding of the United States of America. Rather than force a bitter pill down someone's throat, I have to make Patrick Henry a living, breathing presence for people who never knew he existed or for others who never realized just how critical a figure he was. I'm charged with transporting our guests in a time machine so they can then be challenged by "a most remarkable man," as he was called by his friend Judge Spencer Roane in that deliciously understated 18th century manner.

Generally speaking, actors work from scripts fabricated by playwrights who wish to tell a story about people who never actually lived. The actors work on a stage or a set specially designed to help tell the story, and they rarely have the opportunity to discuss their characters' backgrounds with the playwright.

Charged with the task of making their characters real human beings, which is vital if they are to make the story interesting, they must rely on clues available to them in the dialogue making up the script. Successful actors, therefore, must be able to invent their characters' lives previous to the first words uttered in a scene

This is what actors call "getting into the character's head." Living History actors, or interpreters, also work from scripts, but those scripts are the actual words of their characters written in their own hands. Their clues are real, not imagined. The "scripts" also include newspapers, documents, journals, letters, receipts, inventories, and laws and customs of the age. Our stage at Colonial Williamsburg is the very ground upon which the real Patrick Henry trod. We feel the energies and ghosts of the buildings and landscapes which he felt. Living History interpreters certainly still have to do some invention, but do so based upon extensive research of primary documents relating to people who actually existed, saw it happen, and took the time to write about it. Accuracy is our mantra.

I am convinced that Henry's words, deeds, and principles are essential for the preservation of our republic. They were never more relevant than on that most horrid of days, 11 September, 2001. I was scheduled to do the Publick Audience behind the Governor's Palace at 10:35 AM. While dressing at home, I learned of the first airplane slamming into the World Trade Center. By the time I got to the Palace, reports of the other attacks had come in. Moments before I was slated to take the stage, one of my fellow interpreters tersely informed me that one of the towers had come down. Numbed with shock and sorrow, I made my way to the dais through a large crowd of cheerful, smiling visitors when it dawned on me that they hadn't heard the news. These vacationers had arisen early, gone to breakfast, and hit the streets, eager to hear what Mr. Henry had to say. Did I tell them to seek shelter, the nation was under attack? Or did I recite Mr. Henry's thoughts about the crisis America was facing in 1775?

Perhaps it was cowardice, but I determined to give them the show as advertised, thinking that they'd find out soon enough – it wasn't my proper place to inform them. As I listened to myself, I couldn't believe what I was hearing myself say. It was as if Mr. Henry had taken my body over. His words of the 1770s were actually addressing the circumstances of 9/11. At one point, as just one example, I heard myself intoning his words from the First Grand Congress: "The distinction between Virginians, Pennsylvanians, New Yorkers, and New Englanders is no more! I am not a Virginian, I am an American!" The Pentagon in Virginia, the field in Pennsylvania, and the Trade Center in New York were the places where Americans died that day, while a number of the hijackers took off from Logan Airport in New England. Eerie, no? Thomas Jefferson may have believed that Mr. Henry's contributions at the First Congress were insignificant, but many post 9/11 Americans sure don't think so. Since that day, I have noticed his timeless relevance more and more.

Compared with other Founding Fathers, Patrick Henry was rather inconsiderate to historians, because he was a talker, not a pamphleteer. Unlike his principal detractor, Thomas Jefferson (who labored perpetually to ensure that he would be revered by future generations by saving every scrap of paper upon which he ever scribbled), if Henry did keep journals, he destroyed them, or they were destroyed by fire or flood. His daughters recounted how he would write beautiful poetry, read the verses aloud to his family and, promptly afterwards, slip the poems into the fire, believing that it was unseemly for a statesman such as he to be known as a poet. Happily, though, enough primary source data exists to piece together a real, living, breathing man who can not only interest, but exhilarate, an audience of today.

Naturally, I am always delighted to hear others' scholarly insights into what made Mr. Henry tick.

Which brings me to George Morrow's excellent and thorough studies of Patrick Henry. I am not a lawyer (though I play one on TV). Extant documents prove that Henry was an extraordinary lawyer. But it takes a lawyer to know a lawyer, and thanks to George Morrow's wonderful insights expressed so amusingly in *The Greatest Lawyer*, I am better able to fathom Henry's legal genius, and so may the casual reader just looking for a good time. I might even go so far as to suggest that law professors would be well advised to make *The Greatest Lawyer* required reading for their students. The nature of man does not change and the tactics employed by Henry in the 18th century court-rooms of Virginia would be equally effective today.

Thomas Jefferson's legal abilities – or rather, inabilities – are also explored in the study. I pray that Jeffersonian scholars and groupies will forgive me for being very biased about the Henry/Jefferson relationship explored in such great detail in *Puffing Squirt*. I feel duty bound to defend the integrity of the gentleman I've been living with for 15 years, particularly as he was unable to do so himself. Jefferson, after all, waited until Henry's death before he so viciously maligned the object of his jealousy. Jeffersonians should read this study, the better to understand their man. One can only imagine the bewilderment of Henry's first biographer, William Wirt, when he compared the recollections of Jefferson to those of his other correspondents.

The source of Jefferson's venomous hostility towards Henry has been discussed by other historians, but George Morrow delves into aspects of Jefferson's character that no others have. Were Henry to read this work, he might very well say, "Vindication and redemption at last!"

I'm fairly confident that I have read just about everything

that has been published about Patrick Henry. Most biographies of him give the reader the facts and figures; few come as close to getting into his psyche as do George Morrow's essays. The late Henry Mayer, a Henry biographer, once said that "psycho-analytical history can be dangerous," but George Morrow is thoroughly convincing on Henry as a lawyer, and on Thomas Jefferson as a scoundrel. All too often, biographers present the great orator as a two-dimensional figure, but George Morrow's studies round out Patrick Henry to the full, and I say that as someone who has been "becoming" the man for fifteen years.

RICHARD SCHUMANN
Colonial Williamsburg's Patrick Henry

Richard Schumann as Patrick Henry
Reproduced by permission of the Colonial Williamsburg Foundation

"I make my living by being politically
incorrect and insensitive"

The Speaker's Chair
"It was in the midst of this magnificent debate"

The Greatest Lawyer That Ever Lived

As great moments in history go, Patrick Henry's May 30, 1765 Stamp Act speech calling for a Cromwell to stand up against George III has to rank near the top.[1] It marked the debut of a man whom Thomas Jefferson called "the greatest orator that ever lived."[2] It also gave (again according to Jefferson) the "first impulse to the ball of [America's] Revolution," thereby transforming what had been a largely academic debate over natural rights into a call to arms. Here it is, described with all the bombast that Henry's first biographer, William Wirt, was known for:

> It was in the midst of this magnificent debate, while he was descanting on the tyranny of the obnoxious act, that he exclaimed in a voice of thunder, and with the look of a god – 'Caesar had his Brutus – Charles the first, his Cromwell – and George the third' – 'Treason,' cried the speaker – 'treason, treason,' echoed from every part of the house. – It was one of those trying moments which is decisive of character. – Henry faultered not for an instant; but rising to a loftier attitude, and fixing on the speaker an eye of the most determined fire, he finished his sentence with the firmest emphasis) *'may profit by their example*. If *this* be treason, make the most of it.'[3]

It was a good story. But was it true? Not even Wirt was sure. In fact, he had no sooner written these immortal words than he "began to doubt whether the whole [story] might not be fiction."[4] Having previously secured the assistance of Thomas Jefferson for his "little literary project" and "[w]ith a view to ascertain the truth" from someone who was actually there that day, Wirt decided to submit the tale of Patrick Henry and the Speaker to "Mr. Jefferson as it had been given to me."[5] No matter that 40 years had passed, no matter that Jefferson still bore a grudge against Henry for a 1781 legislative inquiry into Jefferson's inept and, some said, craven conduct as wartime governor of Virginia. Jefferson would decide. And decide he did: "I well remember the cry of treason [Jefferson replied], the pause of Mr. Henry at the name of George the III, and the presence of mind with which he closed his sentence, and baffled the charge vociferated."[6] That was enough for Wirt: "The incident," he declared in a footnote to his *Sketches of the Life and Character of Patrick Henry*, "becomes authentic history."[7]

And so the matter stood until 1921, when *American History Review* published a hitherto unknown eyewitness account of the incident found in the files of the French spy service.[8] The writer of the scholarly introduction to the account noted that the anonymous author seemed to "use English and French with nearly equal freedom, at any rate spell[ed] both about equally well," but since the manuscript was "in the same hand throughout, with the same peculiarities of execution," he concluded that the account "was not the first manuscript, but . . . the result of subsequent copying." More recently, Rhys Isaac has suggested that the first manuscript was in fact the original manuscript and that the "Frenchman" was actually "a disaffected Irish Catholic," writing in his native brogue – thereby explaining why the Speaker's charge of "Treason!" became "traison" in the so-called "copy."[9] As an Irishman, and thus a victim of English tyranny himself, it was natural that the spy would take an interest in a regicidal speech by any of George III's subjects, particularly one with a Scotch-Irish name :

May the 30th. Set out early from halfway house in the Chair and broke fast at York[town], arrived at Williamsburg at 12, where I saw three Negroes hanging at the gallows for having robbed Mr. Walthoe[10] of 300 ps. I went immediately to the assembly which was sitting. . . . Shortly after I came in one of the members stood up and said he had read that in former times Tarquin and Julius [Caesar] had their Brutus, Charles [the First] had his Cromwell and he did not doubt that some good American would stand up for his country, but (says he) in a more moderate manner, and was going to continue, when the speaker of the house rose and Said, he, the last that stood up had spoke traison, and [he, the Speaker] was sorry to see that not one of the members of the house was loyal enough to stop him before he had gone so far. Upon which the same member stood up again (his name is hennery) and said, that if he had affronted the speaker, or the house, he was ready to ask pardon, and he would shew his loyalty to his majesty King G[eorge] the third, at the Expence of the last drop of his blood but what he had said must be attributed to the Interest of his Country's dying liberty which he had at heart, and the heat of passion might have lead him to have said something more than he intended, but, again, if he said anything wrong, he begged the speaker and the houses pardon. Some other members stood up and backed him, on which that affair was dropped.[11]

Speaker John Robinson "The last that stood up spoke traison"

If Patrick Henry baffled (repelled) the charge of treason it was out of the hearing of the Frenchman, whose account of

Henry calling for an assassin for George III at one moment and offering to die for him the next was so matter-of-fact, plausibly *anti*-heroic as to be credible on those grounds alone. Clearly, if what the Frenchman reported was not a complete retraction, it was the closest thing to it. No wonder the affair was dropped. It would be hard to imagine a more abject apology or a less heroic ending.

Was Henry a hero or a coward? Had he roared out defiance to King George III only to swallow his pride and along with it, the title of first mover of the American Revolution? The only scholars who seemed willing to grapple with the issue were Edmund and Helen Morgan. As the Morgans expressed it in *The Stamp Act Crisis: Prologue to Revolution* (1967), "The legend . . . of Patrick Henry pouring forth torrents of sublime eloquence and bidding defiance to the shouts of 'treason!' from all corners . . . may still linger . . . for the schoolboy but is now denied to adults."[12] Though they did not say so, the Morgans clearly viewed the Wirt/Jefferson version of the story as beneath the dignity of history. In any case, it was now ruled out and the French Traveler's version was ruled in as "the only direct road . . . to those critical days when Virginia pointed the way to freedom." A few scholars begged to differ, including Henry biographer Henry Mayer, who took the position that Henry's apology was merely "silky" – an admission that he had "seriously miscalculated." The better view, held by Rhys Isaac, was that his apology was part of the performance – "a tactical retreat that took nothing from the audacity of the speech": "[T]he talk . . . in the taverns . . . when [the] . . . traveler resumed his northward journey was boisterous endorsement of Henry's defiance."[13]

Meanwhile, the public seemed indifferent to the Morgans' offer of a more direct road, suggesting either that the truth did not matter or that Wirt's story was simply too good to be *un*true.

Certainly Wirt himself was under no illusions. As he told his friend St. George Tucker in 1815: "But such a narrative you never saw! Narrative! There is no story in it. It is all disquisition, rant and rhapsody – I wish my name had not been given to the public – O that I could have got the reward for the copyright, without being ever known in the affair. – I foresee that Patrick will be the ruin of my literary name."[14] He was wrong: Patrick Henry was not the ruin of Wirt's name but the making of it. The problem with Wirt's *Sketches* is not that it is all rhapsody. It is that its rhapsodies were put into the mouth of "a blank man, blank burgess and blank governor," and such he appeared even to his biographer.[15]

It is not hard to see why Patrick Henry remains America's least known, least written-about Founder. Wirt's *Sketches* met its author's aim of giving America's youth a hero to emulate.[16] Yet to write Henry's life is to quickly find, as Wirt said, that it is "all speaking, speaking, speaking"[17] – but speaking without the words, there being little in Henry's speeches that can be called genuine. What we think of as Henry's greatest speeches are in fact the bombast of Wirt and later biographers, all determined to live up to Jefferson's description of Henry as the greatest orator that ever lived. If Wirt has the edge in this contest, it is due to his skill in making Henry the exuberant alter ego of himself.

William Wirt
"I foresee that Patrick will be the ruin of my literary name"

That there has been no major biography of Henry in fifty years is not surprising.* The words on Henry's headstone, "His fame is his best epitaph," have been called a "deep irony."

---

* As this book goes to press, Da Capo Press has just published a new biography of Patrick Henry by Harlow Giles Unger entitled *Lion of Liberty*.

Henry's fame, as biographer George Willison has pointed out, "has gone into almost total eclipse."[18] The deeper irony is that Henry was eclipsed from the start, not by popularizers and hacks but by the "gigantic proportions and superhuman qualities" attributed to him by a nation determined to make supermen of patriots even if, as Charles Francis Adams noted, that robbed them "of all their merit."[19] The question is no longer whether Patrick Henry actually uttered the words attributed to him by Wirt. The question is, who *was* Patrick Henry? Was he the greatest orator ever? If so, how did get to be that way?

Patrick Henry was born on May 29, 1736 to an educated Scotch-Irish immigrant from Aberdeen, John Henry, and his wife, Sarah Winston Syme, both members of the Virginia gentry. Henry's uncle, called "Patrick Henry Sr." to distinguish him from his nephew, was an Anglican cleric with an M.A. from Aberdeen's Marischal College who came to America with Henry's father. Though Jefferson professed to believe that Henry had no Latin and even less Greek, it is a fact that John Henry personally tutored his son in Latin, Greek, the Bible and classic works of English literature. (At Patrick Henry's death, his library amounted to 200 volumes, a sizable gentleman's library in a colony in which some aristocrats, the owners of vast plantations, could barely sign their names.) It was Henry's Presbyterian mother, Sarah, who brought him (at the age of eleven) to hear the greatest orator of the age, the Reverend Samuel Davies, preach from a stump in a forest clearing. Attempts to trace Patrick Henry's oratorical ability to this encounter are as inventive as they are clearly strained:

> Regrettably, Henry did not specify what he learned by listening to Davies. Some important similarities between the

popular preacher and the popular politician, however, tease the imagination: a ready utterance, expressed in an exceptionally musical and animated delivery; a plain, pungent style that without seam addressed the understanding and the affections; a keen appreciation of the current exigencies in the audience's experience; the union of patriotism and Christianity; the bold rebuke, even of kings; and the action appeal that was invariably a call for a moral response.[20]

The better view may be that this catalogue of imagined similarities applies at least as well to any experienced trial lawyer and that if there were lay preachers in Henry's family, there were a good many more judges. In fact, by the time Henry was 16, half of the twelve sitting justices on the Hanover County Court bench were his close relatives, with his father, John Henry, often acting as Presiding Justice. The only surprise about Henry's career choice is that he did not set out to become a lawyer from the start.

In fact, his decision to study the law seemed to be mostly the result of desperation. By 1760, Henry had already failed twice as a country shopkeeper and once as a tobacco planter, in the process exhausting the entire dowry brought to him by his 1754 marriage to Sarah Shelton. He was never (as Jefferson claimed) "a barkeeper in a tavern," but he did have to work for a living. And if it is true that a fee was "a necessary preliminary" for Patrick Henry to undertake the defense of the accused, it is also true that the law was an end in itself for Henry in ways that it never was for Jefferson.[21]

Patrick Henry seems in fact to have been a natural lawyer. Unlike Jefferson, he did not study law at the College of William and Mary, nor did he read law with a licensed lawyer. If we are to believe Jefferson, Henry took the bar exam after studying the law for only six weeks. He would have failed it too, except that two of his examiners, Peyton Randolph and George Wythe, passed him on promise alone, while Virginia Treasurer Robert Carter Nicholas (who would turn his practice over to Henry in 1773) passed him only after he agreed to continue with his studies. By 1765, Henry had been a lawyer for only five years; yet he was already viewed as Virginia's best. What is more, he had done it the hard way, accepting and winning the kinds of cases new lawyers usually get – that is, unwinnable cases – and this before he had even completed his legal studies. If it is true, as Jefferson claimed, that Patrick Henry often "ran wild in the field of fact" (and it is), it is because the law had taken the day off or, as lawyers say, "if you don't have the law, argue the facts." Jefferson's oft-quoted charge that Henry was "wholly ignorant of the law," is not only untrue, it is untrue with a motive, being the product of Jefferson's life-long envy of Henry's superiority in the courtroom.

After examining Henry's book of cases and accounts, historian David McCants determined that between the fall of 1760 and the end of 1763 Henry handled a total of 1,185 cases, with "legal advice services and the preparation of out of court papers [being] . . . in addition."[22] Between 1761, his first full year of practice, and 1763, "Henry's [annual] caseload doubled, from about 185 cases to 374 cases. Moses Coit Tyler estimated that Henry handled twice as many cases as Thomas Jefferson did during his first four years of practice. . . . From 1764 to 1786, he handled 2,200 civil and an unrecorded number of criminal suits." By comparison, in 1767, his first full year of practice, Jefferson recorded a total of 68 cases in his casebook, none of which went to trial and 19 of which were administrative proceedings argued before a clerk. Jefferson's accounts for 1767 suggest a motive for his description of Patrick Henry as "avaricious": jealousy. Though he debited clients £183 for services that year,

Jefferson was only able to collect £17 – which means that, after deducting costs and expenses, his net receipts for the year were only £10. As Frank Dewey has noted, "If his costs, including the expenses of four trips to Augusta County and three trips to Williamsburg are considered, he was considerably out of pocket. Even if he had expected an unprofitable first year, Jefferson must have been disappointed at these dismal figures."[23] Nor did the situation get much better as the years passed. By the end of 1774, when he turned over his practice to Edmund Randolph, Jefferson had recorded a grand total of 959 cases, 226 less than Henry handled during his first three years in what was almost entirely a trial practice. Frank Dewey, a lawyer himself, also effectively exploded the sentimental myth of Jefferson's extensive practice in the county courts.[24] In fact, he had no practice whatsoever in these courts. He was barred from them by law, as were all General Court lawyers. During his eight years at the bar of General Court, Jefferson received a grand total of £1,200 in fees, just twice what Paul Carrington, a county court lawyer, made in one year and not even close to the £1,568 earned by General Court lawyer John Mercer in 1764, his last full year in practice. In belittling jury causes and high fees, Jefferson was presumably contending for a law practice focused on administrative proceedings and small fees – in short, a practice much like his own. With that, the defense might rest – except that the point of Jefferson's critique of Henry was not his contemptible irresistibility to juries but his inability to transfer his oratorical skills to his writing.

It is certainly true that Henry was focused on his audience and the spoken word. That did not of course prevent Jefferson from ridiculing his "vulgar and vicious" pronunciation. Nor did it lessen Edmund Randolph's surprise at his trampling of the rules of classic rhetoric.[25] To be sure, none of the surviving sources ever called Patrick Henry "a simple country lawyer."

The Virginia courts were too rule-oriented, its advocates too formal to view that as a compliment. But in fact, artful simplicity and arresting directness will always be hallmarks of the best lawyers.

Both of these traits were on display in the House of Burgesses on May 30, 1765. Prepared though Henry was for the Speaker's outrage, being accused of treason was no small matter. But if his purpose was to remove the offense by simply apologizing for it, he did not succeed. Instead, Henry told the Speaker that "in the heat of passion" he had said more than he intended, an apology that in effect sought to justify treason on the grounds of emotional necessity. To say that he had spoken in "the Interest of his country's dying liberty" did not excuse treason. It was a motive for it. He was not putting the issue to rest. He was making sure he kept it alive, even as he positioned himself in the minds of his audience as spokesman-in-chief for liberty.

Rather than the act of a coward, Henry's apology was the act of a skilled advocate, revealing superlative timing, mental agility and the ability to not only give offense deftly but exploit it. The great revelation of the French Traveler's account, for those prepared to accept its authenticity, is that Patrick Henry Jr. was not only a facile speaker but a very quick mind.

That lawyers sometimes make (and then apologize for) prejudicial outbursts in the course of trial will be clear to anyone who has ever watched a courtroom drama on television. And outbursts – albeit of a much less shocking nature than Henry's – were as common in Virginia courtrooms in 1765 as they are today. The reason is clear. Not all facts are admissible under the rules of evidence; not all arguments will be deemed proper. Knowing that his "jury" of burgesses could not un-hear what he had said, Henry offered his accuser a *"readiness* to ask pardon *if* he had affronted" him – a conditional apology, if it was even that.

His call for an assassin for King George III stood; nothing he said afterwards changed that fact. The question is, was Henry's outburst planned? We cannot be sure. What we can say is that he had done nearly the same thing just two years before.

The occasion was the 1763 trial of the famous Parson's Cause,[26] in which Henry appeared before a jury of his neighbors with his father sitting as Chief Justice. In what can only be described as a dry run of his Stamp Act speech, Henry called George III "a tyrant" and told the jury that if they awarded the plaintiff, an Anglican cleric named James Maury, even a farthing they would "rivet their own chains [and] perpetu-ate their own servitude." Here, too, the room erupted in cries of "Treason!," though this time they came from the spectators. Obviously, Henry was attempting to prejudice a home-town jury against the defendant. Nor was he unwise to do so, Maury's claim being based on the King's veto of an Assembly bill that allowed Virginia's drought-stricken planters to pay the local clergy's stipends in cash rather than tobacco.

King George III
"His call for an
assassin for King
George III stood"

Henry's immediate motive was to achieve professional noto-riety by calling George III "a tyrant" – notoriety being, then as now, a good way to acquire a practice – a point frankly admitted by Henry: "After the court was adjourned, [said Maury] he apol-ogized to me for what he had said, alleging that his sole view in engaging in the cause, and saying what he did, was to render himself popular."[27]

That Henry admitted using a lawyer's trick to make himself popular and poison the jury's mind does not mean that he was dishonest or that he did not speak for his audience. But what it does tell us is that the sly country lawyer was the father of Wirt's orator of nature: that many, if not all of the mannerisms described by observers were actually acquired by Henry in the courtroom. The list of these mannerisms is in fact quite long and easily recognizable to a modern trial lawyer. They include the "unassuming" look and "very respectful" treatment of his opponents that Henry's friend Judge Roane said ensured that "no feeling of disgust or animosity was arrayed against him"; the speech "hobbles" and "simplicity" which "promised little" to a stranger but to an experienced trial lawyer like Edmund Randolph signaled a *calculated* "absence of trick" and a *seeming* lack of "rhetorical artifice." Nor are we surprised to hear that Henry occasionally added a "skeptical smile" to his usual "excess of humility, diffidence and modesty" whenever he was forced to "submit . . . to the superior wisdom of the court."[28]

The approved way to play Patrick Henry, still, is on one's hind legs, in full cry. That is all wrong. Shouting may make for high drama but it is pure death to a trial lawyer. Passionate advocacy is not only painful for a jury to listen to, it almost always sounds false. Edmund Randolph perhaps put it best when he said, "His was the only monotony which I ever heard reconcilable with true eloquence."[29] "[T]he apparent languor of his opening, " said Randolph, "[was] contrived to [make him] be the focus . . . of every person present . . . He transfused into the breast of others the earnestness depicted in his own features, which ever forbade a doubt of sincerity. In others rhetorical artifice and unmeaning expletives have often been employed as scouts to seize the wandering attention of the audience; in him the absence of trick constituted the triumph of nature." Judge Moses Coit Tyler perhaps came closest to describing the complex effects Henry got through monotony when he described to Wirt how a "burst of eloquence from a man so very plain and ordinary," in his first appearance as counsel before the august House of Burgesses' Committee on Privileges and Elections, had "struck the committee with amazement" causing "deep and perfect silence . . . during the speech." [31] The result was a lawyer's dream: "not a sound, but from his lips, was to be heard in the room." By building tension through hesitations and by actually resisting the impulse to rant, Henry was able to combine a sense of great urgency and irresistible power to produce the impact of an intimate revelation.

It was Jefferson, with his talk of "torrents of eloquence," who persuaded Wirt, no mean trial lawyer himself, to render Henry's Stamp Act speech as bombast. Never mind that Wirt's sources were adamant in insisting that Henry "sounded no alarm." [31]

Thus it is that the so-called "evangelical model," the bible-banging style of the Rev. Davies, has gradually replaced the testimony of the men who knew Henry best, his colleagues at the bar. Henry did in fact say that he had learned "what an orator should be" from listening to Davies, and there is no doubt that he liked to sprinkle his speeches with biblical allusions and analogies. [32] But to say that Davies taught him how to be an orator or that he modeled himself after a preacher is to reveal a forgivable but nonetheless profound ignorance of the realities of courtroom practice.

Rev. Samuel Davies
"What an orator should be"

As good as Davies was on a stump or a pulpit, he would have been an utter failure in a courtroom, where the facts reign and the best result is not justice but the far more elusive perception of justice. There is no evidence that Henry did any preaching, unless it was to testify to his faith in church, while, on the other hand, the record is filled with scores of reports from observers, some hostile to Henry, testifying to his irresistibility to juries (Jefferson) and his great ability to sway judges.

The strongest link between Henry and Davies turns out to be in the minds of scholars "teased," as McCants put it, by "important similarities between the popular preacher and the popular politician," on the one hand and "dissatisfying" contemporary accounts that lack "vividness" on the other.[33] If Edmund Randolph's monotonous orator does not exist, it is because we refuse to accept him; because the myth of the stentorian Henry, "Son of Thunder," is too deeply embedded in our minds.

There is another possibility, of course, and it is that Henry was simply a good actor. Though a man of the cloth, Rev. Archibald Alexander was evidently not one to believe in miracles. So sure was he that Henry was a fraud that he decided to attend a hearing in Prince Edward Circuit Court to decide (he said) "whether like a player [Henry] merely assumed the appearance of feeling." Alexander left so struck by the "intensity of feeling" shown by Henry *in requesting a continuance* that "all [his] doubts were dispelled." Henry was "not acting"; his credibility was "instantaneous." But could an advocate who traded knowledge of the law for intensity of feeling still be a great lawyer? If you believed, along with Jefferson, that encyclopedic knowledge of the law is the *sine qua non* of success at the bar – a not implausible notion to many people – your answer might be "he could not." But Jefferson also said that Henry was "impressive . . . beyond what can be imagined. . . . . When he had spoken in opposition to my opinion . . . I myself have been highly delighted and moved."[34]

It was a stunning admission, perhaps forced out of Jefferson by his great age (he was then 81) and by the fact that he was talking to the best trial lawyer of that era, Daniel Webster. Thomas Jefferson, the man whose notes in the case of *Blair v. Blair*,[35] were to supply whole generations of scholars with the last word on Henry's supposed defect as an advocate – that he often "ran wild in the field of fact" – was admitting that his great rival's oratory was impressive beyond his imagination.[36] But why was Jefferson only taking notes in *Blair v. Blair*, one of the biggest cases of his own era? Why was he not up on his hind legs, like the other lawyers, some of the best in Virginia? The answer is, because he was a very bad public speaker and, it seems, an even worse advocate. Jefferson once told John Randolph that he found "contention" – mother's milk to a trial lawyer – more "horrid" than death and, as Joseph Ellis has pointed out, was so averse to public speaking that he gave just two speeches (his inaugural addresses) during his eight years as president.[37] He was taking notes because, besides doing legal research for the defense, that was all he could do. It is always a bit unsettling for an experienced trial lawyer to have to "second chair" as co-counsel. To play the part of research assistant while one's intellectual inferior ignores the law to run wild with the facts would be hard for any lawyer; for Jefferson, the only real scholar in the room, it was almost beyond enduring. Interestingly, Wirt chose not to quote Jefferson on Henry's lack of qualification "for anything but mere jury trials" – perhaps because Wirt, one of the best jury trial lawyers in Virginia, viewed trial work as his profession's highest calling.

Later, in 1769, when Henry joined the General Court bar, Jefferson often appeared opposite to him. He does not say whether he lost to Henry on those occasions, only that he was often "bewitched." What seems to be a penetrating critique of Henry thus turns out to be belied by his greatest critic's bias, disabilities and, finally, his unforced admission that Henry was as successful in bewitching him as he was juries. [38]

What was Henry's secret? Was he all smoke and mirrors as Jefferson suggested? If he did learn his craft in a courtroom, how did he acquire such skills so early in his career? How Henry might have responded to these questions is suggested by a remark he made to a law student he met coming out of Rind's bookstore in Williamsburg with a huge armful of law books. "Study men, Mr. Wormeley, study men!" said Henry, thereby affirming his critic's worst suspicions.[39] What Henry meant of course was that the law is not about statutes and precedents, but what persuades juries; that is, "the proper string to touch."[40]

One cannot read anecdotes of Henry the bewitching advocate and spellbinding orator without at some point concluding that neither term is adequate to explain his powers. Whether he was standing in front of a jury or in the well of the House of Burgesses, Henry left audiences dumbfounded – *quite literally unable to recall what he had just said.* Speaking of Henry's first great address as a trial lawyer in the 1763 Parson's Cause, Wirt wrote,

> I have tried much to procure a sketch of this celebrated speech. But those of Mr. Henry's hearers who survive seem to have been bereft of their senses. They can only tell you, in general, that they were taken captive; and so delighted with their captivity, that they followed implicitly, whithersoever he led them; that, at his bidding, their tears flowed from pity, and their cheeks flushed with indignation; that when it was over, they felt as if they had just awaked from some ecstatic dream, of which they were unable to recall or connect the particulars. It was such a speech as they believe had never before fallen from the lips of man.[41]

With that, Wirt not only marked the limits of his own insight into Henry but those of virtually every Henry biographer for the next 200 years.

One reason to still read Wirt, however, is that he came closer than anyone to capturing Henry's eerie, mind-numbing effect –

an effect comparable to mental possession. Thus, Wirt quotes Henry's law partner John Lyons as saying that "he could write a letter or draw a declaration or plea at the bar, with as much accuracy [when another lawyer was speaking in court] as he could in his office . . . except when Patrick rose to speak; but that whenever he rose, although it might be on so trifling a subject as a summons and petition for twenty shillings, he was obliged to lay down his pen, and could not write another word, until the speech was finished."[42] Wirt attributed this to "the charm of [Henry's] voice and manner and . . . originality of . . . conception."[43] But charm and originality of conception only trivialize the Henry effect. What Lyons was saying was that even other lawyers, long-time friends and colleagues, men who had heard Henry speak hundreds of times, could not concentrate when he rose to speak. Apparently, Henry was not only able to empty Lyons' mind of business but commandeer his will.

That Henry got amazing results in mysterious ways was a common observation. Of his son's speech in the Parson's Cause, John Henry told Judge Winston it was given "without Hesitation or Embarrassment . . . on a Subject, of which I did not think he had any Knowledge."[44] Judge Roane told of a case in which Henry was so persuasive the jury found his client not guilty, despite the fact his guilt had already been decided and the only issue was whether it was murder! Another friend recalled the time when one of Henry's oratorical assaults on the tyrannical "British King and ministry" so *inflamed* spectators sitting in the gallery of the House that they "all at once . . . rushed out. It was at first supposed that the House was on fire. Not so."[45] So fiery was Henry's language that someone ran up and doused the royal flag on the cupola. Judge Roane also recalled his father telling him about going up to hear Henry speak in the House of Burgesses in Williamsburg with a Scotsman named Bradfute, "a man of learning," who became so "enchanted with his eloquence as to have unconsciously squirted tobacco juice from the gallery on the heads of the members, and to have nearly fallen onto the House floor."[46] On another occasion, a thunderstorm broke over the capitol just as Henry was "depicting the awful immensity" of a decision that, he suggested, "the ethereal beings were awaiting with anxiety." Suddenly a peal of thunder shook the building. Henry's audience of veteran politicians "broke up in confusion."[47]

The veracity of these stories is likely to remain a matter of fierce speculation, but what mattered was not their truth, but their ability to convey, as metaphors, the mental state of Henry's audience on the one hand and the power of his oratory on the other. Extrapolating from his awed sources, Wirt insisted that "the fire of [Henry's] . . . eloquence never failed to effect a "mysterious and almost supernatural transformation of appearance" in Henry himself. As Wirt put it, there was "in [his] emphasis," a "peculiar charm the magic of which anyone who has ever heard him will speak . . . but of which no one can give any adequate description. They can only say that it struck upon the ear and upon the heart *in a manner which language cannot tell.*"[48]

Apparently, the color of Henry's eyes were also beyond what language could tell. Though nearly everyone who heard Patrick Henry speak claimed to have felt the power of his eyes "rive" them (Wirt's word), there was, oddly, no agreement as to the color of his eyes![49]

St. George Tucker, who had as many chances to observe Henry's eyes from the clerk's table in General Court as anyone, thought they were "dark gray, not large, penetrating, deep-set in his head; his eyelashes long and black, which with the color of his eyebrows made his eyes appear almost black."[50] Judge Roane was at least equally certain that Henry "had a fine blue eye" – adding for good measure that he also had "an excellent set of teeth."[51] Henry's daughter Sarah finally settled the matter when she told Henry's grandson (and second biographer) William Wirt Henry, "Go out on a perfectly clear day and look up at the sky, and you will have an excellent idea of the color of his eyes."[52]

The confusion over Henry's eyes was to be repeated in confusion over his features. Despite the existence of a number of portraits, no one is sure how Patrick Henry actually looked.

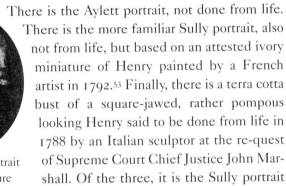

There is the Aylett portrait, not done from life. There is the more familiar Sully portrait, also not from life, but based on an attested ivory miniature of Henry painted by a French artist in 1792.[53] Finally, there is a terra cotta bust of a square-jawed, rather pompous looking Henry said to be done from life in 1788 by an Italian sculptor at the re-quest of Supreme Court Chief Justice John Marshall. Of the three, it is the Sully portrait that seems to fit most people's idea of how Patrick Henry looked. It is of a dark, sharp-nosed Henry posed studio-style eyeglasses atop his head, looking to his left. Sully's Patrick Henry looks more intense, but he is also, at least momentarily, in a state of repose, which is to say he lacks what every Henry portrait clearly must have: the frisson of energy that the orator was said to put into words.

The Aylett Portrait
"No one is sure how Patrick Henry actually looked"

In the end, it is the descriptions of Henry's friends that provide the best portraits. Unlike Wirt who tried to imitate the inimitable, Henry's friends described the man they knew. But the best of these portraits do more than simply describe Henry; they seek to recreate his effect: "Six feet, slight stoop, rather spare, dark complexion, grave countenance, eyes overhung by long lashes and full eyebrows – brilliant, full of spirit, rapid in motion; forehead high and straight; nose somewhat of Roman stamp." The piling up of adjectives, the irruption of a dash in mid-series, all help to render this portrait of Henry kinetically, putting man and features into hypnotic, flickering motion. Another friend achieved similar effects with a description of Patrick Henry's characteristic stoop: "He was rather above than below the common height, but had a stoop in the shoulders which prevented him from appearing as tall as he really was. In his moments of animation, he had a habit of straightening his frame, and adding to his apparent stature" – as if Henry only came to life when he spoke.[54] Disappointed by the inertia in the Sully portrait, another friend explained that it was "necessary to involve [Henry] in some great emergency in order to arouse his more sterling qualities."[55]

A less friendly description of Henry by St. George Tucker suffers in two ways: It was written in Tucker's old age; it was rendered in a style which called for Tucker to balance good impressions against bad, until the desired, cumulative effect of neutrality was achieved – that is, until he got to Henry's mouth, which he described as a font of "cynical or satirical emotion."[56] Tucker, who was once treated (as he believed) rudely by Henry and never forgot it, thought Henry's modesty was put on; his "submissive" smile to the "superior wisdom of the court" purely cynical. As a former clerk of court and an excellent trial lawyer himself, Tucker should have known better. No trial lawyer would be caught dead showing contempt for the judge: the jury will not stand for it, but he might register a wry smile for a boneheaded ruling or a lame argument from opposing counsel. As usual, Henry's good friend and former law partner Judge Roane had it about right. He thought Henry was unassuming to a purpose: to ensure "no feeling of disgust or animosity was arrayed against him."[57]

Judge Roane, who studied Patrick Henry more carefully than most of his friends, ascribed Henry's power over juries to his ability to sense their subconscious impulses and needs. Henry always knew "the proper string to touch," had "a remarkable faculty of adapting himself to his company" and was so indifferent to "rude attacks" he never seemed "even out of temper." Here was an orator who not only studied people, but "made it impossible not to attend to *him*," whose oratory "rose with the subject and exigency," whose "tones of . . . voice . . . matter and gestures were insinuated into the feelings" of hearers "in a manner that baffled all description." "I have likened this faculty of Mr. Henry [added Roane] of operating upon the feelings, whether tragic or comic, by the mere tone of his voice, to . . . ringing a series of glasses by rubbing one of them with the finger. . . . He had a perfect command of a strong and musical voice, which he raised or lowered at pleasure, and modulated so as to fall in with any given chord of the human heart." For Roane, Henry's secret lay in his ability to communicate "bold, strong and striking" ideas in a language "free from unusual or high-flown words," a technique that leveraged his musical voice and "the grandness of his conceptions" for "wonderful effect on the feelings of his audience."[58]

In the end, it was not grand gestures or florid oratory, let alone ranting, that made Patrick Henry seem god-like, but the fact that he left his audience feeling that he had read their thoughts. (Given how closely he watched their eyes, he may have done just that.) Still, while Henry's knowledge of his audience was drawn (as he said) from the study of real men, Judge Roane admitted that he sometimes went over the top, calling up, "spirits from the vasty deep" or echoing the the voices of beings on high with his "eloquent monotone." The last word goes to Edmund Randolph who thought that Henry's use of "figures . . . borrowed from the Scriptures" allowed him to achieve god-like effects by investing himself with the words of God.[59]

We use the term Founder so casually we sometimes forget what we mean by it: a creator of the American nation; a leader, or at least an interpreter, of the American people. Henry's Stamp Act speech is too often viewed (and rendered) as overwhelming sound and fury. What made it the work of a Founder was Henry's ability to voice the inchoate yearnings of an infant nation.

Perhaps too much has been made of the political orientation of Henry's audience. Virginia's back country burgesses did feel resentment toward the local, British-leaning establishment, so it was natural that Henry's call for an American Cromwell would be the talk of the colony. Virginia was a feudal, not a free society, but its constraints applied up and down the social scale. In one sense, all Virginians were oppressed; in another, they were all, directly or indirectly, oppressors of the slaves on which their economy depended. They all toiled on a British fief. In the eyes of George Washington, Virginia was a plantation in which he worked like a slave to produce a product, tobacco, which could only be traded via British factors using British ships and exchanged with British merchants for inferior, second-hand British goods. For many burgesses, rich and poor, Henry's words called to mind a Virginia in which slaves were feared less as a threat of insurrection than a degraded reminder of their owners' bondage. The owners felt pity, but their pity stopped short of giving up what, for many, was the greatest share of their wealth. Add to this a local culture which exalted autonomy and viewed pride as a measure of self-worth, and it is clear why anger at the merest suspicion of British oppression was so intense in Virginia. To be sure, Bostonians who read Henry's resolves in *The Boston Gazette* were as aroused as Virginians. Unfortunately, they missed the punch line: Henry's *viva voce* call for a Cromwell to stand up for his country. The name imported regicide and bloody civil war to the debate, not to express a serious intention to revolt, but to express a sense of wrong so outsized that it permitted slave owners to call themselves "slaves." Henry's Stamp Act speech is thus best seen not as a political statement but as empowering hyperbole, affirming the exceptionalism of both speaker and audience. If, as Gordon Wood has said, the Revolution was "out of all proportion to the stimuli," Henry's ability to express the outrage of an audience of Virginia slave drivers in these terms – that is, as oppressed victims – qualifies him as the most "revolutionary" of all the Founders.[60]

Americans throwing the Cargoes of the Tea Ships into the river at Boston
"Mere milksops compared to the Virginians"

Removed from his place of birth, stripped of his day job as a hard-working trial lawyer and assigned words he never used and impulses he never felt, only to be rejected by scholars as a compound of fact and fantasy, Patrick Henry may be the ultimate object lesson in Founder-olatry. The cure for Wirt's fictions is not Jeffersonian contempt, but recourse to the telling fact and telling eyewitness account that leads us back to the workaday lawyer. By most accounts, America's fight for freedom began on May 30, 1765 in Virginia, a slave colony, when a young Virginia lawyer, a student of men, roared out his anger against a king few had seen except in a print and a country even the most radical Virginian still regarded as "an Eden." Why did Patrick Henry's defiance resonate so powerfully with a Virginia audience of slave drivers? Why did one member of the First Congress describe the Bostonians as "mere milksops" compared to the Virginians?[61] In the end hypnotic oratory can take us only so far in explaining Patrick Henry's appeal.

In *A World Elsewhere*, a book of criticism which aspires to be a cultural study, scholar Richard Poirier described "eccentricities of defiance" in virtually every American writer, from James Fenimore Cooper to Ernest Hemingway. "American books [Poirier wrote] are written as if history . . . can give no life to 'freedom' and as if only language can create the liberated place. The classic American writers try through style temporarily to free the hero (and the reader) from systems, to free them from the social forces which are ultimately the undoing of American heroes . . . . What distinguishes American heroes of this kind . . . is that there is nothing within the real world, or in the systems which dominate it, that can possibly satisfy their aspirations. Their imagination of the self – and I speak now especially of heroes in Cooper, Melville, James – has no economic or social or sexual objectification; they tend to substitute themselves for the world."[62] Thus, we find echoes of Patrick Henry's defiance in the "extravagances of language" used by the blasphemous, god-defying Capt. Ahab in *Moby Dick*, in Huck Finn's fierce refusal to be "sivilized" at the end of *The Adventures of Huckleberry Finn* and even in the marvelous poetry Nick Carraway lavishes on the crook Jay Gatsby in *The Great Gatsby*. All are models of defiance as an "exultation in the exercise of consciousness momentarily set free."[63] All derive their American legitimacy as tropes from mythic impulses first voiced by Patrick Henry. If it is true, as one Virginian said, that British policies had left Virginia in "dissipative indolence,"[64] Henry's inflated defiance, enacted in the King's House, against an oppressive British "tyranny" was a sure winner.

It was not some dour Whig who led his horse out of Williamsburg on April 30, but a man entirely at ease with himself, chatting amiably with a friend – the very picture of self satisfaction. Why had Henry not stayed to protect his resolves from being expunged? Because he had achieved what he came to the capital to do: make a name for himself as an orator; start, not lead a revolution. (After all, the leader of a revolution was not likely to be the first choice of a Virginia gentlemen in search of a lawyer.)

When the painting "Patrick Henry in the House of Burgesses" was unveiled in Philadelphia in 1852, the audience immediately sensed that what they were seeing was "glaringly unlike the original" – so unlike their "settled notions of the orator's appearance and costume." Instead of a "plain and unpretending man" they saw "a well dressed actor" in a "fine scarlet cloak . . . instead of that famous old-fashioned wig which he actually wore at the time, and perhaps twisted awry" (as Henry was said to do when agitated in debate), they were confronted with "'ambrosial curls,' fashionably powdered, and adjusted with nice care and easy

Patrick Henry in the House of Burgesses by P. F. Rothermel "Reimagined from words he never used"

grace about the brow."[65] Did they object to their powdered fraud? Certainly not: by then fiction had become well-accepted fact. A legend in his own time, re-imagined from words he never used, Patrick Henry has yet to go to his reward.

A British Stamp

Notes

1   "Documents: Journal of a French Traveler in the Colonies, 1765," *American Historical Review* (1921), 326: 745.

2   Thomas Jefferson to William Wirt, August 4, 1805, "Jefferson's Recollections of Patrick Henry," contributed by Stan V. Henkels, *The Pennsylvania Magazine of History and Biography* (1910), 34: 387.

3   William Wirt, *Sketches of the Life and Character of Patrick Henry* (Richmond, 1817; Kessinger Publishing Reprint), p.53. (Italics in original).

4   *Ibid.*, p. 53, footnote.*

5   William Wirt to Thomas Jefferson, 23 July 1805, "Jefferson's Recollections," 34: 385–386.; Wirt, *Sketches*, p. 53.

6   Thomas Jefferson to William Wirt, 14 Aug. 1814, "Jefferson's Recollections," 34: 401. In Wirt's *Sketches*, Jefferson's description of "the pause of Mr. Henry at the name of George III," is edited out and replaced by the more stirring account of Henry "falter[ing] not for an instant." In what may be yet another tribute to the tenacity of myth, the elision has gone unnoticed by scholars.

7   Wirt, *Sketches*, p. 53, footnote.*

8   "Journal of a French Traveler," 326: 726.

9   The introduction to the printed journal describes the writer as "a Catholic, and apparently a Frenchman," but notes that "all efforts to identify him . . . have thus far been unsuccessful." "Journal of a French Traveler," 326:726; Rhys Isaac, *Landon Carter's Uneasy Kingdom* (Oxford, 2004). p. 171.

10   Nathaniel Walthoe was Clerk of the Governor's Council.

11   "Journal of a French Traveler," 326: 741–745.

12   Edmund S. and Helen M. Morgan, *The Stamp Act Crisis, Prologue to Revolution* (Williamsburg, 1953), p. 94

13   *Ibid.*, 94; Henry Mayer, *A Son of Thunder Patrick Henry and the American Republic* (Charlottesville, 1991), p. 87; Isaac, *Landon Carter's Uneasy Kingdom*, p. 172.

14 William Wirt to St. George Tucker, August 16, 1815, *William and Mary Quarterly* (July 1913), 22: 250.

15 *Ibid.*, pp. 250–252; Wirt's *Sketches*, p. 54. Love him or hate him, biographers and historians insist on viewing Patrick Henry as a firebrand. But except for his supposed invitation to the Speaker to make the most of his treason (which Wirt rightly suspected of being fiction), Henry was always the model of decorum. Indeed, as Wirt put it in *Sketches*, Henry's "language of passion was perfect. There was no word 'of learned length *or thundering sound*,' to break the charm. It had almost all the stillness of solitary thinking. It was a sweet revery, a delicious trance." Wirt's *Sketches*, p. 58.

16 The book was in its 25th edition by 1871.

17 William Wirt to Judge Carr, 20 Aug. 1815, John P. Kennedy, *Memoirs of the Life of William Wirt: Attorney General of the United States*, (2 vols.; Philadelphia, 1850; Kessinger Publishing Reprint), p. 345.

18 George F. Willison, *Patrick Henry and His World* (New York, 1969), p. viii.

19 Charles Francis Adams to Josiah Quincy, February 9, 1811, Charles Francis Adams, ed., *The Works of John Adams, Second President of the United States*, (10 vols.; Boston, 1850–56), 9: 630.

20 David A. McCants, *Patrick Henry, The Orator* (Westport, Ct., 1990), p. 30. McCant's analysis of Henry's oratorical abilities is among the best. That said, his attempts to derive the great orator's speaking style from the example of Rev. Davies suffers from the usual faults: the regret over the lack of specifics ("Regrettably, Henry did not specify . . ."); followed by the author's stated preference for similarities that "tease the imagination" over documented sources, leading to a Wirt-like, rhapsody that is rich in superlatives without being rich in insight ("exceptionally musical and animated delivery; a plain, pungent style").

21 Thomas Jefferson to William Wirt, April 12, 1812, *The Works of Thomas Jefferson in Twelve Volumes*, Paul Leicester Ford, ed., http://memory.loc.gov/cgibin/query/r?ammem/mtj:@field(DOCID+@lit(tj110097)) (accessed 5/15/2008).

22 McCants, *Patrick Henry, The Orator*, p. 96

23 Frank L. Dewey, *Thomas Jefferson, Lawyer* (Charlottesville, Va., 1986), p. 34.

24 *Ibid.*, "Appendix B: The Myth of Jefferson's County Court Practice," pp. 122–126.

[25] Edmund Randolph, *History of Virginia* (Charlottesville, Va., 1970), p.213.

[26] The Parson's Cause was an action brought by the Rev. James Maury to collect back stipends due him as a result of the King's veto of the Two Penny Act of 1758. To quote David McCants: "The . . . Act . . . authorized that debts due in tobacco could be paid in cash at the rate of eighteen shillings per hundred pounds of tobacco. The purpose of the law was to avert the economic hardship that a short tobacco crop portended. Since tobacco was a common medium of exchange for private and public obligation, the Two Penny Act directly affected all segments of Virginia Society. Under the act, the Anglican clergy would receive substantially less than the value of 16, 0000 pounds of tobacco inflated by the poor harvest but more than the usual cash value of their salary. Nevertheless, the clergy, already disgruntled and threatened by society's poor regard for them and the weak status of the established church, protested." McCants, *Patrick Henry, Orator*, pp. 37–38. Henry could not win the case, as the King had already vetoed the Act. The only question remaining was how much the clergy should be paid in the way of back stipends. Henry got what we would now call "a defense verdict." Instead of awarding Rev. Maury £288 pounds, the amount he was owed, the jury, egged on by Henry references to the clergy as "rapacious harpies," awarded him a mere two cents.

[27] James Maury to Rev. John Camm, quoted in William Wirt Henry, *Patrick Henry: Life, Correspondence and Speeches*, (3 vols.; 1891) I: 43–44. On the subject of how a young lawyer should go about acquiring a practice, Wirt advised his first wife's younger brother, Francis Walker Gilmer, to "Get yourself, either by a fee, or voluntarily, into the most important cause that is to be tried in Winchester, in the fall term . . . . *level yourself* to the *capacity of your hearers*, and insinuate yourself among the heartstrings, the bones and marrow, both of your jury and back-bar hearers." (Italics in original) William Wirt to Francis Gilmer, July 23, 1815, quoted in Gregory K. Glassner, *Adopted Son: The Life, Wit & Wisdom of William Wirt, 1772–1834*, (Madison County, Va., 1997), p. 112. All very good advice. Wirt was also a believer in the use of rhetorical tricks: "speak slowly, distinctly, and mark your periods by proper pauses, and a steady significant look – 'Trick!' True – but a good trick and a sensible trick." *Ibid.*, p. 113.

[28] "Judge Spencer Roane's Memorandum," Appendix B, George Morgan,

The True Patrick Henry (1907; Reprint, American Foundation Publications, 2000), pp. 121–122 (quoting St. George Tucker) and 444; Edmund Randolph, *History of Virginia* (Charlottesville, Va., 1970), p. 180.

[29] Edmund Randolph, *History of Virginia*, p. 180;

[30] Quoted in Morgan, *The True Patrick Henry*, p.76.

[31] *Ibid.*

[32] Quoted in McCants, *Patrick Henry, The Orator*, p. 30.

[33] *Ibid.*

[34] Quoted in Morgan, *The True Patrick Henry*, p. 383; McCants, *Patrick Henry, The Orator*, p. 30; Fletcher Webster, ed. *The Private Correspondence of Daniel Webster,* (Boston 1857 [University of Michigan Reprint]), p. 367.

[35] The case of *Blair v. Blair*, in which Lord Dunmore, as Chief Judge of the Virginia General Court, affirmed the right of his mistress, Catherine ("Kitty") Eustace Blair to one half of the estate of her deceased husband, James Blair, is the centerpiece of *A Cock and Bull for Kitty*, the first booklet in this series.

[36] Frank L. Dewey, "Thomas Jefferson and a Williamsburg Scandal: The Case of *Blair v. Blair*," *Virginia Magazine of History and Biography* (1981), 89: 44–63, see also, Frank L. Dewey, "Thomas Jefferson's Notes on Divorce," *The William and Mary Quarterly*, (Jan. 1982), p. 39.

[37] Thomas Jefferson to John Randolph, 25 Aug. 1775, *The Thomas Jefferson Papers Series 1. General Correspondence. 1651–1827*, http://hdl.loc.gov/loc.mss/mtj.mtjbib000114 (accessed 9/22/2010); Joseph Ellis, *American Sphinx: The Character of Thomas Jefferson* (New York, 1996), p. 225

[38] Webster, ed., *Private Correspondence of Daniel Webster*, p. 367. Why Jefferson was such a poor trial lawyer would make a very interesting book.

[39] Quoted in Morgan, *The True Patrick Henry*, pp. 211–212.

[40] Quoted in Morgan, *The True Patrick Henry*, p. 448.

[41] Wirt, *Sketches*, p. 26. That Wirt's *cri de coeur* came on page 29 of a 296 page book may explain some of his dismay.

[42] Wirt, *Sketches*, p. 32. (Italics in original.)

[43] *Ibid.*

[44] "Judge Edmund Winston's Memoir of Patrick Henry," quoted in Wirt, *Sketches*, p. 25.

[45] Quoted in Morgan, *The True Patrick Henry*, pp. 136–137.

[46] *Ibid.*, p. 442.

[47] *Ibid.*, p. 447. "[I]t seemed," said Judge Roane, as if Patrick Henry was

actually "calling up spirits from the vasty deep."

48 Wirt's *Sketches*, p. 24.

49 Wirt's *Sketches*, p. 287.

50 Quoted in Morgan, *The True Patrick Henry*, p. 121.

51 *Ibid.*, p. 454.

52 *Ibid.*, p. 120. As late as 1907 one biographer (George Morgan) was still grousing that "all do not agree as to the color of [Patrick Henry's] eyes" – leaving us with this question: why, given the fact that Henry had riveted his "determined eye" on thousands of enraptured listeners was there ever any doubt? See Morgan, *The True Patrick Henry*, pp.120–121.

53 The attestor was none other than John Marshall, first Chief Justice of the U.S. Supreme Court. But see also the "Memorandum" of Henry's good friend Judge Roane: "The miniature shown by Mr. Wirt has some resemblance of Mr. Henry, but is not a good likeness." "Judge Spencer Roane's Memorandum," Morgan, *The True Patrick Henry*, p. 454.

54 Both of the above quotations appear in Morgan, *The True Patrick Henry*, p. 119.

55 *Ibid.*, p. 123.

56 *Ibid.*, pp. 121–122.

57 *Ibid.*, p. 444.

58 *Ibid.*, pp. 436, 445, 447.

59 Randolph, *History of Virginia* , p. 180.

60 Gordon Wood, *The Creation of the American Republic*, 1776–1787 (Chapel Hill, NC, 1969), p. 3.

61 Morgan, *The True Patrick Henry*, p. 157, (quoting Joseph Reed, a delegate from Pennsylvannia).

62 Richard Poirier, *A World Elsewhere* (Oxford, 1966), p. 5.

63 *Ibid.*

64 Jack P. Greene, ed., *The Diary of Landon Carter*, (2 vols; The Virginia Historical Society, Richmond, 1987), 1 : 512.

65 Morgan, *The True Patrick Henry*, p. 99 footnote* (quoting the Virginia *Historical Register.*)

Monticello in 1825
"He reserves is abhorrence for the arcana of a certain snug sanctuary"

Patrick Henry
and the Puffing Squirt

History may distort truth, and will distort it
for a time, by the superior efforts at justification
of those who are conscious of needing it most.
The opening scenes of our present government
will not be seen in their true aspect until the
letters of the day, now held in private boards,
shall be broken up and laid open to public view.[1]

Thomas Jefferson, 1823

Among chroniclers of what he has described as the "duplicity"
of Thomas Jefferson, Joseph Ellis stands out, both for his
insightful analyses of his subject and his genial acceptance of
the hostility that seems to go with being Jefferson exposer-in-
chief. In *American Sphinx*, Ellis compares Jefferson's enmity for
Patrick Henry to his hatred of Alexander Hamilton and finds
that Henry, like Hamilton, "was a youthful prodigy of impover-
ished origins . . . whose visible cravings for greatness violated
the understated code of the true Virginia aristocrat. To make
matters worse, Hamilton as an opponent was equally formida-
ble on his feet and in print." Like Jefferson, Henry and Hamilton were lawyers; unlike Jefferson, they did not fear con-
frontation. How did a shy, scholarly lawyer deal with conflict? If
his name was Jefferson, he went to ground. "Cautious and shy,"
was how Hamilton described him in 1792, "wrapped up in
impenetrable silence and mystery, he reserves his *abhorrence* for
the arcana of a certain snug sanctuary [Monticello], where

seated on his pivot chair, and involved in all the obscurity of political mystery and deception ... he circulates his poison thro' the medium of [Phillip Freneau's Republican newspaper] *National Gazette*." [2]

The comparison between Hamilton and Patrick Henry is apt for another reason. If Jefferson disliked Alexander Hamilton, he was truly obsessed with taking revenge on Henry whom (he said) "had inflicted a wound on his spirit" that "only the all healing grave" could cure.[3] Jefferson was convinced that Henry had orchestrated a Virginia Assembly inquiry into his inept and seemingly cowardly conduct as Governor of Virginia during the British invasion of 1780–81. Even worse for Jefferson than the thought of Henry's five term record of success in the same job[4] was the mortifying recollection of Henry's dominance in Virginia political and legislative affairs. In a 1784 letter, Jefferson asked James Madison – in code – to "devoutly pray" for Henry's death. At other times, Jefferson described Henry as "implacable," "a great foe" and a potential dictator seeking "every power . . . over our persons."[5] If Jefferson's vocabulary for Henry reminds us of the monsters in the old sagas it is because Henry inspired in Jefferson a deep, archetypal loathing. For most Virginians, Patrick Henry would remain the revered defender of their country's liberties. For Jefferson, he was a threat to both country and ego; a would-be despot and usurper of his peace of mind.

Jefferson's bedroom at Monticello
"Seated on his pivot chair . . .
he circulates his poison"

Given the number of times that Jefferson has been quoted on the subject of Henry's "torrential" eloquence it seems strange that no one has trained Jefferson's metaphor on himself. Though Jefferson's dislike for Henry is well known, its verbal texture has been largely ignored. To call the same man "the best humored man . . . I ever knew" and "avaricious & rotten-hearted,"[6] in adjoining sentences in the same letter is, at the very least, to reveal a high tolerance for paradox — to exhibit, as Joseph Ellis has noted, an "impulse to invent and then embrace . . seductive fictions."[7] In truth, Jefferson hated Henry; hated him so much that anything good he had to say about Henry should not only be viewed with skepticism but as a warning to be on guard for duplicity to follow. Thus, when Jefferson told Daniel Webster in 1824 that he was often overawed by Henry the orator he was actually marking the end of a successful 21-year effort to obliterate all memory of Henry the man.

The vehicle he had used, William Wirt's extraordinarily popular *Sketches of the Life and Character of Patrick Henry* (1817), was probably not the one he would have preferred. That said, no one was more adept in the use of mouthpieces to destroy his enemies than Jefferson. In 1805, he secretly paid the yellow journalist James Callendar to libel his old friend John Adams. In 1806, he persuaded a credulous young Virginia protégé, Sen. William Branch Giles, to initiate a senatorial investigation of Alexander Hamilton's financial dealings as Secretary of the Treasury. But unlike Jefferson's hirelings and tools, Wirt owed him no duty beyond that of respect, a situation that greatly complicated Jefferson's efforts to infuse the life of Henry with malice.

Wirt's *Sketches* turned out to be a both a personal and a commercial success, celebrated by both critics and the public alike, and going to 25 editions in the course of 64 years. Readers who were pleased to discover they had been given an authentic America hero to emulate, were even more delighted to find that he had the imprimatur of another American hero:

Jefferson. Furthermore, Jefferson did not stint in his praise, calling Henry "the greatest orator that ever lived."[8] While it would be unfair to describe Jefferson's praise for Henry's oratory as entirely disingenuous, it would also be unjust to allow Jefferson the last word on Henry's greatness as a man and orator. Having seduced Wirt with extravagant praise for Henry it was relatively easy for Jefferson to get Wirt to bury his rival under enough bombast to justify the title "the greatest orator that ever lived." The reader who summed up his reaction to Wirt's *Sketches* as "HENRY'S eloquence and that of Wirt /The roaring torrent, and the puffing squirt!" could thus be said to speak for Thomas Jefferson as well.[9]

Scholars have yet to fully analyze Jefferson's effect on Henry's place in history. Meanwhile Wirt's Henry, described by his creator as "all rant and rhapsody," has been condensed into a few speeches, only to be condensed again into his most famous ripostes, including his fictitious reply to Speaker Robinson's cry of "Treason!": "If this be treason make the most of it!"[10] The fashion for reducing Henry to a few words has led at last to the attenuation of the man himself, so that now all that most people can recall about Patrick Henry is "Give me liberty or give me death!"[11] Jefferson would be pleased. "A fitting epitaph," he would probably say, "and in his own words, too!"

What biographer George Willison in 1969 called the "deep irony" of the words on Patrick Henry's grave, "His fame is his best epitaph," has been succeeded by an "almost total eclipse" of Henry the man.[12] Meanwhile, as David McCants has noted, scholars continue to make liberal use of Wirt's fictions, decrying their falsity even as they seek to dress them up "with fictionalized versions" of their own.[13] In the greatest irony of all, the man who hated Henry the most has become the chief authority for his greatness.

What follows is the verbal equivalent of an archeological dig on disturbed ground, which is to say ground rearranged to cover the tracks of the first man on the site: Thomas Jefferson. So closely connected is Jefferson to Patrick Henry that his very impulses are now part of our truth: from the inflated praise for the orator that left the known facts of the man shadowed in disbelief, to the maledictory summing up of Henry's celebrity ("no man can be happy . . . till he is dead")[14] that ensured Henry would always be seen as a crude first draft of speeches as recalled by Jefferson. Suffice it to say that the life of the truly great man Jefferson tried to destroy has yet to be written, not for lack of materials, but because his foremost detractor has taught us to ignore their plain truth: that the greatest orator was also the greatest man in what is still inaptly called "Thomas Jefferson's Virginia."

The collaboration that was to ultimately decide Patrick Henry's place in history began rather innocently with a July 23, 1805 letter from Wirt seeking materials for a "little literary project":

Dear Sir,

In this intermission of your public labors [Jefferson's first term as President had just ended] I hope there may be nothing improper in begging the aid of your memory towards a little literary project which I have on foot. I am collecting memoirs of the late Patrick Henry. His life and example appear to me to afford some fine lessons. His faults as well as his virtues will be instructive, and I propose to myself to be his biographer; not his panegyrist. I find much difficulty in collecting materials such as will enable me to render this work interesting. The materials which I collect are too general and jejune; there is nothing in them which brings me near to the character of Mr. Henry or which will enable me to bring my reader so.[15]

Would Jefferson, who had endured so much from the "perfidy and treachery of man," be willing to trust Henry's first biographer "with free communications concerning [his subject]?"[16] In describing himself as an intimate friend of one of Jefferson's favorite nephews, Wirt hoped to assure him that he could:

> From the very little indeed that you know of me; I feel considerable difficulty in that to . . . [your nephews] I am intimately known. If you find their report of me such as I anticipate, you will believe the assurance which I now give you *on my honor*, that any communication which you shall be pleased to confide to me, shall be seen by no eyes, but my own, and that they shall be returned to you as soon as I have used them. I am peculiarly anxious on this subject because I know, from your thorough acquaintance with Mr. Henry, that information so minute, authentic and interesting as you could give would be alone sufficient to stamp the highest value on my work. (Italics in the original.)[17]

Wirt was offering Jefferson more than a promise of secrecy. He was offering him anonymity. What is more, he was offering it on his italicized *honor,* framed in assurances that Jefferson's stamp would be of the highest value as the mark of what was factual, authentic and interesting. Not all of that was flattery. Jefferson had known Henry for more than thirty years. Moreover, as he later told Wirt, he had "witnessed the part [Henry] bore in nearly all the great questions."[18]

Yes, Jefferson, replied, he "could recollect some anecdotes not uninteresting"[19] – the trailing double negative having less to do with the promise of interesting tales to follow than with his need to reflect carefully on how to exalt the hero without immortalizing the man. Later, Jefferson would tell Wirt that his observations were "mere suggestions, meant to recall the subject to a revision by [him]self," subject to "the confirmed dictates of [Wirt's] own judgment." To the direct testimony of a party to all the great questions was thus to be added the cachet of a President, yet Wirt was to allow no "foreign ingredient" to adulterate "the genuine character of his composition." [20]

Here was a chance for Jefferson to not only decide Henry's place in history but to determine it in relation to his own, all apparently without fear of contradiction or attribution. Jefferson lost no time in taking advantage of it. His first installment in what was to be a 12-year correspondence on the subject of Henry was written within three days of his receipt of Wirt's letter. Mere suggestions or not, they have been the point of departure for every Henry biography for the last 200 years:

Monticello Aug. 4 [1805]

Dear Sir:
Your favor of July 24 [sic] has been duly received: and I feel every disposition to comply with your request respecting Mr. Henry: but I fear to promise from a doubt whether my occupations would permit me the time to recollect and commit to paper the facts respecting him which were within my own knowledge; as we had a very familiar intercourse for upwards of 20 years, & ran our course nearly together. During this our political principles being the same, we acted in perfect concert until the year 1781. I witnessed the part he bore in nearly all the great questions of that period, & perhaps could recollect some anecdotes not uninteresting. He was certainly the man who gave the

first impulse to the ball of revolution. Were I to give his character in general terms, it would be of mixed aspect. I think he was the best humored man in society I almost ever knew, and the greatest orator that ever lived. He had a consummate knowledge of the human heart, which directing the efforts of his eloquence enabled him to attain a degree of popularity with the people at large never perhaps equaled. His judgment in other matters was inaccurate, in matters of law it was not worth a copper: he was avaricious & rotten hearted. His two great passions were the love of money & of fame: but when these came into competition the former predominated. If the work you propose is not destined to come out speedily I will endeavor to recollect what may be of use to it. Be assured I want the testimony of nobody as to the honorable use you would make of my communications. Accept my friendly salutations & assurances of sincere esteem & respect.

Th. Jefferson[21]

Clearly, Jefferson intended to rely fully on Wirt's assurances of confidentiality and anonymity. Just as clearly, his letter presented Wirt with a dilemma: interested though he might be in getting Jefferson's stamp and dedicated though he was to showing Henry's faults, bad judgment and avarice were hardly proper material for a hero worthy of emulation by America's youth.

Why he and Henry had parted ways in 1781, Jefferson did not say. Nor did Wirt, for all his familiarity with the perfidy of Jefferson's enemies, ever try to reconcile Jefferson's abhorrence for Henry the man with his wistful memory of an era of "perfect concert."[22] The failure of Wirt, throughout his correspondence with Jefferson, to realize that he had become the instrument of another man's revenge may be one of the most poignant ironies in American letters. Jefferson would later tell Wirt that he did not finally set down his recollections of Henry until 1810. There were reasons for this, not the least of which was Wirt's failure to get on with his great project. But Jefferson also needed time: time to reflect; time to calibrate the effect of mixing veneration and vengeance.

In the meantime, both men got on with their lives: Jefferson to finish his second term as President of the United States; Wirt to build on an already successful career in the law. Born in 1772 to a family of innkeepers, orphaned at eight and licensed to practice law at twenty, Wirt was to enjoy a degree of professional success and literary fame that comes to few lawyers. In 1800, he helped defend Jefferson's friend James Callendar on Alien and Sedition Act charges. In 1806, he won an acquittal for George Wythe Sweeney for poisoning his uncle George Wythe, a case that must have been as painful to Jefferson (Wythe was Jefferson's friend and mentor), as it was undoubtedly important to Wirt's future career as a national politician. In 1807, he prosecuted Aaron Burr in the treason show-trial of the century, losing the case but delivering an opening speech that is still viewed as a model of legal eloquence. Meanwhile, his *The Letters of a British Spy* (1803) was earning him fame as a political satirist. All Wirt seemed to lack to make him happy was money, and it was money (along with a desire to give America's youth someone to emulate) that finally prompted him to revive his project on Patrick Henry.

On January 18, 1810 Wirt wrote again to Jefferson, reminding him of his promise, as a witness to the great events of 1776, to supply him with interesting anecdotes of Patrick Henry. "[S]o great is the inconsistency of the statements which I have received of his life and character, and so recent and warm the prejudices of his friends and his adversaries, that I had almost brought my mind to lay aside the project as one too ticklish for faithful execution at the present time."[23] That Wirt expected him to resolve the inconsistencies in Henry's character, Jefferson clearly saw. Thus, when he replied to Wirt's letter in March of 1810, it was to tell him that though his memoir of Henry was "now in hand & advanced" "it *will be* written in the supposition that it is to be entirely confidential."[24] What Wirt had offered as an assurance was thus transformed, by a Jeffersonian legalism ("written in the supposition") into what lawyers call "a contractual condition precedent." Even so, Wirt did not receive Jefferson's memoir of Henry until April of 1812, two years later. Why had Jefferson taken two years to send a paper promised in 1805? He tried to explain: "The enclosed paper written for you a year or two ago, has laid by me with a view still to add something to it, but on reflection, I send it as it is. The additional matter contemplated respected Mr. Henry's ravenous avarice, the only passion paramount." Whether Jefferson was reflecting on saying more, or (as seems more likely) afraid that he had said too much, remains an open question. His immediate occasion for writing was however clear: he wanted Wirt to quash a subpoena served on him as the executor of the estate of his old friend Arianna Randolph. For a man who hated conflict, even to be called as a witness in a probate matter was upsetting.[25] As he told Wirt, "A love of peace and tranquility, strengthened by age and a lassitude of business, renders it extremely disquieting to me to be harassed by vexatious lawsuits by persons who have no earthly claim on me, in cases where I have been merely acting for others."[26] So it happened that the promised anecdotes of Patrick Henry became a retainer meant to secure the blessings of its author's tranquility.

What Wirt thought when confronted by Jefferson in the full flower of his malice we can only imagine. We do know that he became so "despair[ing] of the subject" that the life of Henry was henceforth the "sketches . . . of Henry," and that what might have been insights into America's least known founder were now merely "lessons in eloquence." The project, Wirt told Jefferson,

> has been continually sinking under me. The truth perhaps cannot be prudently published by me during my life. I propose at present to prepare it and leave the manuscript with my family. I still think it an awful subject and one which may be advantageously wrought not only into lessons on eloquence, but on the superiority of solid and practical parts over the transient and gaudy show of occasion. I wish only it had been convenient to you to enable me to illustrate and adorn my scheme by a short portrait of Mr. H's most prominent competitors. I have given you too much trouble tho' already to seek to give you more. I need only add the prayer which is on my heart that Heaven may crown your future life with that perfect peace to which, if man ever was, you are so justly entitled. [27]

True to his vow of secrecy, Wirt never did disclose the malicious character of Jefferson's memoir. Failing to fully grasp the insidious nature of Jefferson's praise, many historians have done the same. Others, disarmed by Jefferson's seemingly candid admission of its mixed character, have sought to transform the progressively downward trajectory of his memoir into something like a balanced critique. Meanwhile, the first and best reading of the document – Wirt's "sinking" feeling – has gone largely unnoticed.

Jefferson told Wirt he had laid by his letter "with a view still to add something," only to send it "on reflection, as is." Did he think he had been too hard on Henry? Not at all. He was thinking of adding more about Patrick Henry's "ravenous avarice, his paramount passion." [28] And why had he not added more?

He did not say. But something he said in a later letter to Wirt – that it was best not to print some of the more salacious rumors about Henry as they might be *refuted* – suggests that artful silence was as much a part of Jefferson's attack on Henry as outright slander and that the very phrases scholars have relied on to show Jefferson's fairness are hedged and qualified by malice.

In his memoir of Henry, Jefferson traced their acquaintance to a Christmas 1760 encounter at the home of Col. William Dandridge. Jefferson was then 17; Henry was 23. Both men were headed for Williamsburg: Jefferson to begin the reading law under the guidance of George Wythe at the College of William and Mary; Henry to take his bar examination. When they met up again in the capitol, Henry told Jefferson that he had only studied six weeks for the bar – a display of boyish bravado that Jefferson elected to take as proof of a lack of aptitude. As Jefferson put it, "two of [Henry's] examiners, Peyton & John Randolph . . . signed his license with as much reluctance as their dispositions would permit them to show. Mr. Wythe absolutely refused. Rob[ert] C[arter] Nicholas refused also at first, but on repeated importunities & promises of future reading, he signed."[29] Jefferson claimed to have elicited "these facts" from the gentlemen themselves, the two Randolphs "acknowledging [that Henry] was very ignorant of law, but that they perceived him to be a young man of genius & did not doubt that he would soon qualify himself."[30] That Henry had in fact later qualified himself brilliantly as a lawyer not even Jefferson could deny. But he did deny, vigorously, that Henry's later appointment to the General

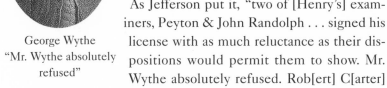

George Wythe
"Mr. Wythe absolutely refused"

Court bench was merited, Henry being in Jefferson's eyes "totally unqualified for anything but mere jury causes." Nor was Jefferson surprised that his avaricious colleague had focused mainly on criminal business where the threat of capital punishment made it easy to squeeze "poor devils" for fat upfront retainers. Jefferson simply could not admit that the size of Henry's fees was a fair reflection of his abilities – or that a fat retainer in capital cases (so notably absent from his own accounts) was the rule rather than the exception in Virginia.[31]

In Jefferson's view, Henry's "transcendent eminence as an Orator & Statesman" [32] was as absurd as it was baffling: absurd because Henry lacked Jefferson's academic qualifications; baffling because innate ability could not possibly account for Henry's mysterious power as an orator:

> In ordinary business he was a very indifferent member. He could not draw a bill on the most simple subject which wd bear legal criticism, or even the ordinary criticism which looks to correctness of style & ideas, for indeed there was no accuracy of idea in his head. His imagination was copious, poetical, sublime, but vague also. He said the strongest things in the finest language, but without logic, without arrangement, desultorily. This appeared eminently & in a mortifying degree in the 1st session of the 1st Congress which met in Sep 1774.[33]

With that, Jefferson changed the subject: from Henry's poetical oratory to his own, finer prose; from Henry's mortification in the 1774 Congress to a flattering comment by New York delegate Robert Livingston regarding Jefferson's essay *A Summary View of the Rights of British America*, (1774). "I think it," he quoted Livingston as saying, "the first composition in the English language."[34] The contrast between his own superlative prose and Henry's oratory was left to speak for itself. But it spoke loudest of Jefferson's need to make Henry a faint echo of the greatness of Jefferson. The final judgment was of course never in doubt: Patrick Henry was a bad lawyer and a worse man.

Jefferson told Wirt that he merely wished to limit Henry's fame to a "sufficiency." "To claim questionable merits [he explained] detracts [from] . . . the estimate of [Henry's] character,"[35] as if post mortem attacks on Patrick Henry's mental abilities were somehow in his best interest! In the court of Jefferson, talk of the defendant's dubious merit often precedes passing of sentence. And that is what happens here, as in the very next sentence we find Jefferson insisting that Henry's "apostasy" (his supposed betrayal of republicanism) "sunk him to nothing, in the estimation of his country." Jefferson's final judgment on Henry is as inevitable as the generally downward arc of his critique. Instead of a summing up, we are given a series of increasingly negative phrases that trace Henry's descent:

[H]e lost at once all that influence which federalism had hoped, by cajoling him, to transfer with him to itself, and a man who, through a long & active life, had been the idol of his country, beyond any one that ever lived; descended into the grave with less than its indifference, and verified the saying of the philosophers, that no man can be called happy till he is dead.[36]

As if consigning Henry to ignominy were not enough, Jefferson then summons up the ghost of George Washington to bear witness to a scurrilous tale of his betrayal by his old friend Henry, said by Jefferson to have "expressed more than any man in the U. S. his thorough contempt and hatred" for Washington because he had campaigned for "adopting the new [U. S.] constitution in 1788."[37] While it was true that Henry was "violently opposed" to the Constitution, it is also true that he deeply admired and respected Washington. As is so often the case with one of Jefferson's lies, the "well known" fact – Henry's opposition to the Constitution in principle – is exaggerated into *"violent* opposition" to the Constitution and all its supporters, thereby adding a spurious "weight" to an otherwise totally false charge of personal "hatred" for the Constitution's greatest supporter: George Washington. Jefferson knew how shocking Henry's betrayal would sound to Wirt, just as he knew that there was no one alive who could – or would – refute the judgments of a former president, mere suggestions or not.

George Washington "Summoned to bear witness to a scurrilous tale of his betrayal"

Given the scope and intensity of Jefferson's efforts to destroy Patrick Henry, it may seem absurd to charge him with encouraging Wirt to turn his work into a panegyric. A different picture emerges, however, when one examines his entire correspondence with Wirt. In his first letter to Jefferson, Wirt had spoken of his "difficulty in collecting materials such as will make the work interesting" and bewailed his inability to get "near to the character of Henry."[38] He seemed even further away five years later, having received so many "inconsistent statements" "filled with the recent and warm . . . prejudices of [Henry's] friends and his adversaries," that he was thinking of "lay[ing] aside the project as one too ticklish for faithful execution at the present time."[39] To Wirt's implied question as to whether he should abandon the project, Jefferson said nothing – a rare example of seeming restraint, were it not so clearly designed to serve his ultimate purpose. That someone would write Henry's life, Jefferson had no doubt; nor did he object to it being Wirt. What he wanted, what Wirt had promised him, was the opportunity to direct its course as a work-in-progress.

Meanwhile, weighed down by illness and a busy law practice, Wirt slogged on, eventually reaching, as he wearily told his friend, Judge Carr on August 20, 1815, his "one hundred and seventh page."[40] Remarkably, his view of Patrick Henry and the difficulty of writing about his life had not changed:

> Now for Patrick Henry. I have delved on to my one hundred and seventh page; up-hill all the way, and heavy work, I promise you; and a heavy and unleavened lump I fear me it will be, work it as I may. I can tell you, sir, that it is much the most oppressive literary enterprise that ever I embarked in, and I begin to apprehend that I shall never debark from it without 'rattling rope and rending sails.' . . . I thought I had [the facts] all ready spread out before me; a pile of old journals on my right, and another of old newspapers on my left, thinking that I had nothing else to do but, as Lingo says, 'to saddle Pegasus and ride up Parnassus.' Such short-sightedness is there in 'all the schemes o' mice and men'; for I found, at every turn of Henry's life, that I had to stop and let fly a volley of letters over the State in all directions, to collect dates and explanations, and try to reconcile contradictions. Meanwhile, until they arrived, 'I kept sowing on.'
>
> In the next place, this same business of stating facts with rigid precision, not one jot more or less than the truth – what the deuce has a lawyer to do with truth! To tell you one truth, however, I find that it is entirely a new business to me, and I am proportionately awkward at it; for after I have gotten the facts accurately, they are then to be narrated happily; and the style of narrative, fettered by a scrupulous regard to real facts, is to me the most

difficult in the world. It is like attempting to run, tied up
in a bag. My pen wants to perpetually career and frolic it
away. But it must not be.

+ + + +

Tertio: The incidents of Mr. Henry's life are extremely
monotonous. It is all speaking, speaking, speaking. 'Tis
true he could talk: – 'Gods! How he could talk!' but there
is no acting 'the while.' From the bar to the legislature,
and from the legislature to the bar, his peregrinations
resembled, a good deal, those of some one, I forget whom,
– perhaps some of our friend Tristram [Shandy's] characters, 'from the kitchen to the parlour, and from the parlour
to the kitchen.' And then, to make matters worse, from
1763 to 1789, covering all the bloom and pride of his life,
not one of his speeches lives in print, writing or memory.
All that is told me is, that on such and such an occasion he
made a distinguished speech. Now to keep saying this
over, and over, and over again, without being able to give
any account of what the speech was, – why, sir, what is it
but a vast, open sun-burnt field without one spot of shade
or verdure? My soul is weary of it, and the days have come
in which I can say that I have no pleasure in them. I have
sometimes a notion of trying to the plan of Botta, who has
written an account of the American war, and made
speeches himself for his prominent characters, imitating,
in this, the historians of Greece and Rome; but I think
with Polybius, that this is making too free with the sanc-
tity of history. Besides, Henry's eloquence was all so
completely *sui generis* as to be inimitable by any other: and
to make my chance of imitating him still worse, I never
saw or heard him. Even the speeches published in the

debates of the Virginia convention are affirmed by all of my correspondents, not to be his, but to fall far short of his strength and beauty.

✦ ✦ ✦ ✦

Again: there are some ugly traits in H.'s character, and some pretty nearly as ugly blanks. He was a blank military commander, a blank governor, and a blank politician, in all those useful points which depend upon composition and detail. In short, it is verily, as hopeless a subject as man could well desire. I have dug around it, and applied all the plaster of Paris that I could command; but the fig tree is still barren, and every bud upon it indicates death instead of life. 'Then, surely, you mean to give it up?' On the contrary, I assure you, sir: I have stept in so deep that I am determined, like Macbeth, to go on, though Henry, like Duncan, should bawl out to me, 'Sleep no more!' I do not mean that I am determined to publish. No sir; unless I can mould it into a grace, and breathe into it a spirit which I have never yet been able to do, it shall never see the light.

Judge Carr being a friend, Wirt was free to go on at length about the "blankness" of his subject and his own inability, despite his pen's tendency to frolic, to breathe life into a "lump." For all his natural ebullience, Wirt was clearly worried, and not only about the fate of his book. He had agreed with publisher Charles Webster to write a 300-page biography of an orator whose words were lost and whose life, so far as it was known, could actually be summed up in a few pages. That Wirt would have to make up many of Henry's greatest speeches had been clear from the start. What was not clear was the extent to which "ugly traits in H's character" – nearly all of which were supplied by Jefferson – and the supposed blanks in Henry's life would require him to fictionalize. There was a possibility, he told St. George Tucker, that he would be caught in a lie and that readers would think his life of Henry was "compounded" out of "old newspapers":[41]

Richmond, August 16th 1815

Give me joy, give me joy! I am in my ninety-sixth page and shall finish my hundredth before I get my hero to the head of his regiment in '76. Now the deuce is in it, if I can't spin fifty pages more out of the sequel of his life, and compound 150 pages of appendix out of the Journals and old newspapers, and behold here will be the 300 complete!

O. Brains, Brains! Help me out of this scrape, and if ever I tax you again with such another task, 'Spit in my face, and call me horse!' But such a narrative you never saw! Narrative! – There is no story in it – it is all disquisition, rant and rhapsody – I wish my name had not been given to the public – O that I could have got the reward for the copyright, without being ever known in the affair. – I foresee that Patrick will be the ruin of my literary name. In trying to save him from the jaws of time, I shall lose myself to eternity. . . What must be done in such a matter. You, Cabell and Monsieur must pass upon it for me before it goes out of my hands . . . It was part of my plan to append a sketch of the characters with whom Mr. Henry acted in '65 – I had seen none of them, except the wives of Pendleton and Wythe – Yet I drew the Speaker Robinson, Peyton Randolph, Richard Bland & Richard H. Lee, all in the dark – but as there was some danger that a few characters might be living, who would be able to catch me in a lie (a most inconvenient thing) I sent these characters to Mr. Jefferson to set me right if I was

wrong. His words in reply are – 'Your characters are inimitably (mark that, Sir, inimitably, — say inimitably) and
justly drawn.' I sent them to him indeed to see if they
were justly drawn, but when I found they were inimitably
drawn, I did not care so much about the justice.

Wirt was clearly not joking when he told Tucker that he did not
care so much about the justice of his characters after Jefferson
told him they were "inimitably drawn." As he told Judge Carr,
the need to state facts with rigid precision had given him trou-
ble from the start, turning what might have been, figuratively
speaking, a dash up Parnassus into an clumsy attempt to run
tied up in a bag.[42] Meanwhile, Jefferson was continuing to supply Wirt with increasingly vicious anecdotes of Henry. Thus, in
the same letter in which Jefferson described Wirt's rendering
of key Virginia characters as inimitably drawn he also described
Henry's manners as "coarse" and his disposition as "idle."[43]
Jefferson's effusive praise for Wirt's characters did not make his
attacks on Henry more credible, but it did not make them any
less credible and the fact that the man Wirt was relying on to
tell him what was true had decisively stated that Henry was
worthless could not have made it easy for him.

Buoyed by Jefferson's praise for his characters, but still
believing that he would be "damned" by a public "predisposed
to dash my thimbleful of reputation from my lips," Wirt decided
to send Jefferson the first 92 pages of his manuscript – all he had
completed to date.[44] This time the question of whether he
should publish was front and center, with Jefferson to be the
judge. Wirt put it this way: "When I was engaging with Webster,
last summer, with respect to the publication, I refused expressly
to bind myself to furnish it at any particular period, – foreseeing
the extreme uncertainty as to the time of the completion, from
the interference of professional duties, and wishing to reserve

to myself, also, full leisure, to revise, correct, and retrench at pleasure. But he has made such an appeal to my humanity, on account of the expensiveness of the materials which he has laid in for the publication, that I am much disposed to let the work go, in its present general form, if you think it can be done without too much sacrifice."[45] Wirt made sure Jefferson understood what he asking:

> What I mean is this, that I think the whole work might be recast to advantage. But then, it must be written wholly anew, which would ill suit Webster's alleged situation; my disposition, therefore, is to let the form of the work remain, correcting the composition, statements, etc, where it shall be suggested and thought proper.
>
> If you think the publication of the work will do me an injury with the public, I beg you to tell me so, without any fear of wounding my feelings. I am so far from being in love with it myself, that I should be glad of a decent retreat from the undertaking. I confide implicitly in your frankness and friendship, — and beg you to believe me, dear sir, with the greatest respect and affection,
>
> Your friend and servant,
>
> Wm Wirt

Wirt would treat a "no" from Jefferson as decisive. All that he needed was a decent retreat from the undertaking. But if Jefferson should find the manuscript merely in need of revision, he hoped that at least he would not have to write it wholly anew, a hope shared by every would-be author since time began.[46]

In the event, Jefferson vastly exceeded Wirt's expectations. He not only read the manuscript through with much pleasure; he actually used it to correct errors in his own memory of events:

Dear Sir, I have read with great delight the portion of the history of Mr. Henry which you have been so kind as to favor me with . . . and I can say from my own knowledge of the contemporary characters introduced into the canvas, that you have given them quite as much luster as themselves would have asked. The exactness too of your details has in several instances corrected the errors in my own recollections where they had begun to falter. In result, I scarcely find anything needing revisal. Yet to shew you that I have scrupulously sought occasions of animadversion, I will particularize the following passages which I noted as I read them.[47]

What Wirt had once called a "rant" was now transformed by the lodestone of Jefferson's delight. There was one thing Jefferson did want softened however: the description of Henry "reading Livy thro' once a year."[48] "He may have read him *once*, [declared Jefferson] and some general history of Greece; but certainly not twice." His basis for this statement? "[T]he learning ascribed to [Henry] in this passage would be inconsistent with the excellent and just picture given of his indolence thro' the rest of the work." The artful circularity of this was also typical of Jefferson. Having convinced Wirt that Henry was lazy and incapable of sustained thought, Jefferson now proposed to offer Wirt's own "just picture" of Henry's indolence as authority for the notion that Henry was too lazy to read Livy! By now, the pattern of Jefferson's editorial suggestions and Wirt's responses was well established: For the accuracy and style of Wirt's *Sketches of Patrick Henry* Jefferson had only high compliments. For the successful lawyer, statesman and popular governor that was Wirt's subject he had only disdain. Forced to choose between the great orator and the inferior man, Wirt naturally opted for the mythic orator. Meanwhile, Wirt was under unrelenting pressure from Jefferson to say more and more about less and less.

The arrival of more galleys on September 2 gave Jefferson a chance to issue a final correction. He had read the galleys, he told Wirt, "with the same avidity and pleasure as the former . . . they need but little, or rather I should say nothing."[49] That was not altogether true. Jefferson was becoming worried that the book might be "too flowery for the sober taste of history." As Jefferson said in a July 26, 1816 letter to a friend: "True history, in which all will be believed, is preferable to unqualified panegyric in which nothing is believed."[50] Was Jefferson worried that Wirt's portrait of Henry was too flowery – a rhapsodic rant, as Wirt put it – or too implausible? If it was too florid, both mythic orator and would-be panegyrist would be written off as windbags; too unbelievable and the call might go out for someone to rescue Patrick Henry from William Wirt. At the same time, any hint of Henry as the fearless wartime governor was sure to get a rise out of Jefferson, who never heard of Henry's conduct in that office without thinking of himself, and it did now. "[T]hat Mr. Henry wanted personal courage," he told Wirt, "was the very general belief of all his acquaintances, strengthened perhaps by inference from the fact that his brother William, and half brother Syme, were notorious cowards. But I know nothing of the facts on which this opinion . . . was founded."[51] So what was the point of mentioning it? Did Jefferson expect Wirt to damn Henry as a *coward* on the basis of "general belief," attributed to no one and "strengthened" by an "inference?" Was he simply passing on something he had heard, with a proper caveat as to its possible untruth? Was he being devious or candid? You can never tell with Jefferson where Henry is concerned, but given the heretical nature of the charge, admitting that it might not be founded in fact was surely the least he had to do if he expected to retain his Wirt-given status as the principal authority for Henry's greatness.

What followed was a dialogue between Jefferson's two minds, rare for having survived to a final draft and rarer still as evidence of the subtlety of his efforts to manipulate the historical record. The subject was how Wirt might plant an "undying" hint of Henry's cowardice in readers' minds: "[B]ut [wrote Jefferson] since this trait in Mr. Henry's character has at least been believed and no fact has been produced to prove it ill-founded (for his march to Williamsburg proved civil courage only, but not military, as he knew there was no enemy to meet him) why bring it into view at all?"[52] Was he worried about making Wirt an accomplice to slander? Not at all. He was worried "that if this point be urged it may produce contradiction and proof, which would die away if not excited." How much better to let rumor continue to circulate than to give Henry's friends a chance to refute it! There was also a chance, were Wirt to publish the rumor, that it would be traced back to Jefferson himself, in which case he might experience something he claimed to dread even more than death: conflict. The charge and countercharge of healthy debate were not Jefferson's way; insinuation and intrigue were.

For his part, Wirt was ecstatic. Replying to Jefferson's September 4 letter, he wrote, "I can tell you with very great sincerity, that you have removed a mountain-load of despondency from my mind, by the assurances that you could find entertainment in these sheets." Again, he entreated Jefferson "not to spare your remarks on account of the defacement of the manuscript. I had rather commence it *de novo* than lose the advantage of your freest criticisms. If you think the narrative too wire-drawn, or the style too turgid – points about which I have, myself, strong fears – I depend on your friendship to tell me so. Much better will it be to learn it from you, in time to correct it, than from the malignity of reviewers."[53] On the 23rd of October, 1816 Wirt sent Jefferson all the remaining sheets of his life of Patrick Henry. Once again, he raised the issue of whether the book would make a "shipwreck of what little reputation I possess as a writer," and specifically asked Jefferson whether "he would advise him, as a friend, to publish."[54]

This time, Jefferson gave Wirt his unequivocal approval: "You ask if I think your work would be the better of retrenchment? By no means. I have seen nothing in it which could be retrenched but to disadvantage. And again, whether, as a friend, I would advise its publication? On that question, I have no hesitation – on your own account, as well as that of the public. To the latter, it will be valuable and honorable to yourself." Only on the "difficult question" of whether a book purporting to be someone's "life" should show his less attractive side as well as his good side was Jefferson more cautious: "You have certainly practiced rigorously the precept of *de mortuis nil nisi bonum*. This presents a very difficult question, whether one only, or both sides of the medal should be presented. It constitutes perhaps the distinction between panegyric and history. On this opinions are so much divided and perhaps may be so on this feature of your work. On the whole however you have nothing to fear, at least, if my views are not very different from the common, and no one can with more truth give you assurances of great respect & affectionate attachment. Th: Jefferson."[55]

Why did Jefferson want Wirt to publish the life of a man who had sunk to nothing? In his own words (never the last word with Jefferson) because it would be valuable to the public. How a panegyric that said nothing about the real Patrick Henry could be valuable he failed to say. Nor did Jefferson explain how fictionalized speeches could give a true sense of Henry's eloquence. As Wirt said, the harder he tried to pump rhetorical life into Henry, the blanker he seemed. His failed effort to give his readers the real Patrick Henry thus converged with Jefferson's efforts to give them a Henry so heroic it would destroy any hope of the man being remembered for what he was. The problem was not simply that Wirt lacked an authentic text for Patrick Henry's greatest speeches. The problem was that what text he had failed to measure up to "the greatest orator that ever lived," forcing him, at Jefferson's urging, to engage in ever more strenuous efforts to imitate the inimitable. And the matter of Jefferson's influence does not end there, as nearly every biographer since Wirt has felt more or less obliged to imitate the puffing squirt doing Patrick Henry the torrential orator. The result is just what Jefferson hoped for: despite the existence of many authoritative sources on his character and oratory Patrick Henry remains unknown to most Americans.

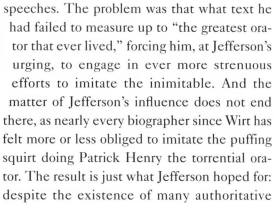

Thomas Jefferson
"As handsome a concession as he ever made"

In December 1824, just 18 months before his death, Thomas Jefferson was visited by the greatest lawyer of the era, Daniel Webster. Though Webster was a firm Federalist and Jefferson a Republican, they quickly developed an intimacy, and it was not long before Jefferson was offering his views on his old rival Patrick Henry. Much of what Jefferson had to say was not true or not new: Henry was "originally a barkeeper" (not true), who received his law license only after "many promises of future study" (not new). Only in the context of a rhapsody could Jefferson accept Henry as his leader in inspiring the American Revolution. But perhaps that was acceptance enough:[56]

Daniel Webster
"They quickly developed an intimacy"

He was as well suited to the times as any man ever was, and it is not now easy to say what we should have done without Patrick Henry. He was far before all in maintaining the spirit of the Revolution. His influence was most extensive with the members from the upper counties, and his boldness and their votes overawed and controlled the more cool or the more timid aristocratic gentlemen of the lower part of the state.

+ + + +

After all, it must be allowed that he was our leader in the measures of the Revolution, in Virginia. In that respect more was due to him than any other person. If we had not had him we should probably have got on pretty well, as you [i.e. the New Englanders] did, by a number of men of nearly equal talents, but he left us all far behind.

Assuming that Jefferson was accurately quoted, it is as handsome a concession as he ever made – a concession which incidentally revealed yet another reason for his malice toward Patrick Henry. It was his being "before all in maintaining the spirit of the revolution," the fact that more of the credit for inspiring the move toward independence had gone to Henry than any other Virginian, including Thomas Jefferson.[57]

The baroque confection of envy, hatred and fear that Jefferson put on display whenever he was asked to talk about his old rival had its source in a fear of domination. Wirt's sources all agreed that Patrick Henry had had an overwhelming effect on audiences. He was said to leave them feeling awestruck, whether in court or in the House of Burgesses, not merely dumbfounded, but quite literally unable to recall what he had just said. Speaking of one of Henry's speeches, Wirt wrote, "I have tried much to procure a sketch of this celebrated speech. But those of Mr. Henry's hearers who survive seem to have been bereft of their senses. They can only tell you, in general, that they were taken captive; and so delighted with their captivity, that they followed implicitly, whithersoever he led them; that, at his bidding, their tears flowed from pity, and their cheeks flushed with indignation; that when it was over, they felt as if they had just awaked from some ecstatic dream, of which they were unable to recall or connect the particulars. It was such a speech as they believe had never before fallen from the lips of man."[58] Nor was Jefferson himself exempt from this effect: "When he had spoken in opposition to my opinion," he told Daniel Webster in 1824, "and I was myself . . . highly delighted and moved, I have asked myself when he ceased, 'what the d[evi]l has he said?' I could never answer the inquiry."[59] In praying for Henry's death, Jefferson had simply expressed his fear of being overwhelmed, or swept away by the sheer force and energy of the greatest orator that ever lived.

And what about poor Wirt's *Sketches?* "His biographer," Jefferson told Webster, "sent the sheets of his work to me as they were printed, and at the end asked for my opinion. I told him it would be a question hereafter, whether his work should be placed on the shelf of history or of panegyric. *It is a poor book written in bad taste, and gives so imperfect an idea of Patrick Henry, that it seems to show off the writer more than the subject of the work.* [Italics supplied.]"[60]

Though Jefferson said Wirt's *Sketches* showed off Wirt more than his subject, he did not say why. Nor did he indicate the very considerable part he had played in ensuring that it did just that. Lacking facts, lacking a real-life drama and being convinced by Jefferson of Henry's ugly traits, Wirt had turned his sketches of the life of Patrick Henry into a demonstration of his own eloquence. What drama there is in the *Sketches* is in the language, as Wirt, in lieu of facts and hoping to give the public a hero to admire, seeks to do the impossible: write the life of a man *too great for words*. A pattern thus firmly established by Henry's first biographer has proved hard, if not impossible to break by succeeding generations of writers.

It is again Joseph Ellis who reminds us of the need for American historians to "dive into the messy moments of [the Founding] and do our best to listen as a finite number of long dead men struggle to understand the historical currents of their rather propitious time."[61] Greatly contributing to the messiness of these moments was the Founders' deep obsession with securing a place in history – what Douglass Adair (quoted by Ellis) has called their "lust for fame"[62] That Jefferson meant to live on "in the memories of subsequent generations as yet unborn" is clear; that he meant to bar Henry from the same place by reviling him in his letters to Wirt is also clear. What may not be clear is the extent to which Wirt's panegyric has helped him to achieve that aim. Of course, Jefferson could not have known how generations unborn would view Wirt's *Sketches*. But he was aware of the distinction between panegyric and history and surely foresaw the destructive effect an absence of fact and larger-than-life standing would have on future portrayals of his rival. No doubt Jefferson savored the irony of arranging for the mythic orator to become a victim of his own myth.

The time is long past for a proper life of Patrick Henry. The incredible speaking hulk crafted by Wirt at the ungentle urging of Thomas Jefferson has prevailed for far too long. Since Wirt, we have had *The True Patrick Henry, Son of Thunder* and just plain *Patrick Henry*.[63] We have had the aspiring dissenting preacher; what we have not had is the supreme trial lawyer, a man who learned how to be an orator not from other orators but – literally – from trial and error. Henry's mannerisms as a lawyer, all noted by reliable observers, might tell a would-be biographer something about the source of his powers, except we all know Henry was fit only for jury causes, not a "real" lawyer like Thomas Jefferson – just as we know that Henry's oratory was indescribable. Henry's surviving letters might tell us something about his ideas and the workings of his mind, except that Jefferson tells us that Henry was a poor writer and how could a poor writer have a great mind? Indeed, anything that might suggest mental agility or presence of mind in Henry has been ruled out of order to be replaced by this or that tale of the speaking fool as imagined by Jefferson and Wirt. We should not be surprised that "the life of Patrick Henry" (who-ever he was), has assumed the status of a subversive delusion, as otherwise sensible scholars try to imitate what they cannot describe.

Local rivalries, even ones as bitter as this, are hardly unusual in American history. What seems unusual about the rivalry between Thomas Jefferson and Patrick Henry – besides its apparent one-sidedness – is its compatibility with the nature of the society in which they lived. Jefferson's efforts to destroy Henry's reputation by commandeering his life have a counter-part in Henry's own efforts to overwhelm Jefferson and other Virginians with torrents of sublime oratory. Hatred of domi-nance and the struggle for dominance are not contradictions in colonial Virginia. They "run" (as Jefferson the property lawyer might have said) with the land of a slave colony, infecting every-one with a passion for liberty and a paranoia about becoming *someone else's* slave. It is not necessary to believe that Jefferson actually plotted to subvert Williams Wirt's little literary project. It is only necessary to believe that he unleashed the impulses within him as a native-born Virginian. But for the fact that he is the most artful of all the founders, this might have been appar-ent long ago. If there is any truth to William Wirt's *Sketches*, it is in what they offer as a window to the soul of Virginia.

Notes

1   Thomas Jefferson to William Johnson, 12 Jun. 1823 Paul Leicester Ford ed., *The Writings of Thomas Jefferson*, (10 Vols.; New York, 1892–1899), 10:228.

2   Joseph Ellis, *American Sphinx, The Character of Thomas Jefferson* (Vintage Books, New York, 1998), p. 153.

3   Thomas Jefferson to James Monroe, 20 May 1782, Julian P. Boyd et al., eds., *The Papers of Thomas Jefferson*, (25 vols. to date; Princeton, 1950), 6: 184–186.

4   Patrick Henry was governor of Virginia during the following years: 1776–1777, 1777–1778, 1778–1779, 1784–1785 and 1785–1786.

5   Thomas Jefferson to James Madison 8 Dec. 1784, *The Republic of Letters, The Correspondence between Thomas Jefferson and James Madison 1776–1826, Vol. I 1776–1790*, James Morton Smith, ed. (W. W. Norton & Co., N.Y., 1995), 1: 353–354; Thomas Jefferson to Gouverneur Morris, 26 Nov. 1790, *The Thomas Jefferson Papers, Series 1. General Correspondence. 1651–1827*, http://memory.loc.gov/cgi-bin/query/ P?m tj:22:./temp/~ammem_TKqy:: (accessed 11/1/2007). On the two "projects" for appointing a dictator in revolutionary-era Virginia, see Thomas Jefferson to William Wirt, 14 Aug. 1814, "Jefferson's Recollections of Patrick Henry," contributed by Stan. V. Henkels, *The Pennsylvania Magazine of History and Biography*, (1910), 34: 402.

6   Thomas Jefferson to William Wirt, 4 Aug. 1805, "Jefferson's Recollections," 34: 386–387.

7   Ellis, *American Sphinx*, p. 38.

8   Thomas Jefferson to William Wirt, 4 Aug. 1805, "Jefferson's Recollections," 34: 387.

9   Quoted in Gregory K. Glassner, *Adopted Son: The Life, Wit & Wisdom of*

William Wirt, 1772–1834 (Chapel Hill, NC, 1997), p. 84

10 William Wirt, *Sketches of the Life and Character of Patrick Henry*, (1817; Kissinger Publishing Reprint), p. 53.

11 *Ibid.*, p. 94

12 George F. Willison, *Patrick Henry and His World*, (New York, 1969), p. viii.

13 David A. McCants, *Patrick Henry, The Orator* (Westport, Ct., 1990), p. 111.

14 Thomas Jefferson to William Wirt, 4 Aug. 1805, "Jefferson's Recollections," 34: 396.

15 William Wirt to Thomas Jefferson, 23 July 1805, "Jefferson's Recollections," 34: 385–386 .

16 *Ibid.*

17 *Ibid.* (Italics in original)

18 Thomas Jefferson to William Wirt, 4 Aug. 1805, "Jefferson's Recollections," 34: 387.

19 *Ibid.*

20 Thomas Jefferson to William Wirt, 29 Sep. 1816, "Jefferson's Recollections," 34: 411.

21 Thomas Jefferson to William Wirt, 4 Aug. 1805, "Jefferson's Recollections," 34: 387.

22 So powerful was Jefferson's prejudice against Henry that even his grammatical faults seem encrypted with animosity: Was Henry "the best humored man" Jefferson *almost* knew or *almost* the best humored man? *Ibid.*

23 William Wirt to Thomas Jefferson, 18 Jan. 1810, *The Papers of Thomas Jefferson, Retirement Series, Vol. 2, 16 November 1809 to 11 August 1810*, J. Jefferson Looney, *et al.* eds., (Princeton and Oxford, 2005), 2: 155.

24 Thomas Jefferson to William Wirt, 25 Mar. 1810, *The Papers of Thomas Jefferson*, Looney, *et al.* eds. 2: 314.

25 If Jefferson wanted to avoid conflict, agreeing to serve as executor in the estate of Arianna Randolph, wife of John Randolph, known as "John Randolph the Tory" to distinguish him from the patriotic members of his family, was a bad place to start.

26 Thomas Jefferson to William Wirt, 12 Apr. 1812, *The Papers of Thomas Jefferson*, Looney, *et al.* eds., 4: 597.

27 William Wirt to Thomas Jefferson, 15 Apr. 1812, *The Papers of Thomas Jefferson*, Looney, *et al.* eds., 4: 615.

28 Thomas Jefferson to William Wirt, 12 Apr. 1812, *The Papers of Thomas*

Jefferson, Looney, *et al.* eds., 4: 597.

29 Thomas Jefferson to William Wirt, 4 Aug. 1805, "Jefferson's Recollections," 34:390. In Jefferson's 1824 interview with Daniel Webster, the name of Edmund Pendleton is substituted for that of Robert Carter Nicholas.

30 *Ibid.*, 34: 387–388.

31 *Ibid.*, 34: 394. As one of the most sought-after criminal lawyers of his era, Wirt might easily have set him straight. That he did not do so, we can put down to his respect for Jefferson – and his need for anecdotes of Patrick Henry. But it does leave a modern lawyer wondering at Jefferson's naivete about one of the most common practices of his profession.

32 Thomas Jefferson to William Wirt, 29 Sep. 1816, "Jefferson's Recollections," 34: 413.

33 Thomas Jefferson to William Wirt, 4 Aug. 1805, "Jefferson's Recollections," 34: 390.

34 *Ibid.*, 34: 392.

35 Thomas Jefferson to William Wirt, 29 Sep. 1816, "Jefferson's Recollections," 34: 413.

36 Thomas Jefferson to William Wirt, 4 Aug. 1805, "Jefferson's Recollections," 34: 395–396.

37 Thomas Jefferson to William Wirt, 4 Aug. 1805, "Jefferson's Recollections," 34: 395.

38 William Wirt to Thomas Jefferson, 23 July 1805, "Jefferson's Recollections," 34: 385.

39 William Wirt to Thomas Jefferson, 18 Jan. 1810, *The Papers of Thomas Jefferson*, Looney, *et al.* eds., 2: 155.

40 William Wirt to Judge Carr, 20 Aug. 1815, John P. Kennedy, *Memoirs of the Life of William Wirt, Attorney General of the United States*, (2 vols; Philadelphia, 1950), 1: 344–346.

41 William Wirt to St. George Tucker, 16 Aug. 1815, quoted in William Wirt Henry, *Patrick Henry: Life, Correspondence and Speeches* (3 vols.; New York, 1891).

42 William Wirt to Judge Carr, 20 Aug. 1815, Kennedy, *Memoirs of the Life of William Wirt*, 1: 344.

43 Thomas Jefferson to William Wirt, 5 Aug. 1816, "Jefferson's Recollections," 34: 408.

44 William Wirt to Judge Carr, 12 Jan. 1816, Kennedy, *Memoirs of the Life of William Wirt*, 1: 352.

45 William Wirt to Thomas Jefferson, 24 Aug. 1816, Kennedy, *Memoirs of the Life of William Wirt*, 1:361–362.

46 *Ibid.*

47 Thomas Jefferson to William Wirt, 4 Sep. 1816, "Jefferson's Recollections," 34: 409.

48 *Ibid.* In Jefferson's 1824 interview with Daniel Webster, it is not Livy but Plutarch that Henry was supposed to have read only once a year.

49 Thomas Jefferson to William Wirt, 29 Sep.1816, "Jefferson's Recollections,"34: 411–413 .

50 Thomas Jefferson to Joseph Delaplaine, 26 July 1816, *The Thomas Jefferson Papers, Series I, General Correspondence, 1651–1827*, Library of Congress Online, http://memory.loc.gov/cgibin/query/P?mtj:17:./ temp /~ammem_nKQS: (accessed 9/23/2010.)

51 Thomas Jefferson to William Wirt, 29 Sep.1816, "Jefferson's Recollections,"34: 412–413,

52 *Ibid.*

53 William Wirt to Thomas Jefferson, [Sept. 12 – Oct. 8, 1816?], Kennedy, *Memoirs of the Life of William Wirt*, 1: 363.

54 William Wirt to Thomas Jefferson, Oct. 23 1816, Kennedy, *Memoirs of the Life of William Wirt*, 1: 363–364.

55 Thomas Jefferson to William Wirt, 12 Nov. 1816, "Jefferson's Recollections," 34: 417–418.

56 "Patrick Henry," Fletcher Webster, ed. *The Private Correspondence of Daniel Webster*, (Boston, 1857; University of Michigan Reprint), p. 368.

57 *Ibid.*

58 Wirt's *Sketches*, p. 26. That Wirt's *cri de coeur* came on page 26 of a 296 page book may explain some of his frustration.

59 Webster, ed., *The Private Correspondence of Daniel Webster*, p. 367.

60 *Ibid.*

61 Ellis, *American Sphinx*, p.58

62 *Ibid.*

63 George Morgan, *The True Patrick Henry*, (New York, 1907; Reprint, Bridgewater, Va., 2000); Henry Mayer, *A Son of Thunder: Patrick Henry and the American Republic* (Charlottesville, Va., 1991); Norine Dickson Campbell, *Patrick Henry: Patriot & Statesman* (Old Greenwich, Ct., 1969).

A Few Words on Virginia Slavery and the Revolution

This is a series about a battle with irony as fierce as the Revolutionary War itself. It is also a series about the overwrought narratives Virginians fashioned to avert those ironies. Some of the Virginians' narratives – those in their letters, for example – were ostensibly private. Others, like Patrick Henry's speeches, Arthur Lee's Monitor essays, George Mason's *Declaration of Rights* and Thomas Jefferson's *Summary View of the Rights of British America* and the American Declaration of Independence, bear all the marks of full-dress theatrical performances. Whether they were speaking to an audience of one or a hundred, Virginians never forgot they were addressing posterity.

Edmund Morgan has said that Revolutionary-era Americans "allowed Virginians to compose the documents that founded their republic, and they chose Virginians to chart its course."[1] That is true. But if Jefferson's Declaration of Independence put words to the visioning of America it also imported to that vision as subtext the defining fact of life in Virginia: black African slavery. Slavery is not listed among Jefferson's self-evident truths. This was after all political propaganda. But the fact is, without slavery, Jefferson would not have had the time or the leisure to imagine America.

This is not to give slavery credit as the atrocity which "sensitized" Virginians to the blessings of liberty.[2] It is however to

---

[1] Edmund Morgan, *American Slavery, American Freedom* (New York, 1975), p. 387.

[2] See Robert Middlekauff, *The Glorious Cause* (Oxford, 1982), p. 606

remind ourselves that nothing in 18th Century Virginia is conceivable without slavery. Slavery supplied white Virginians with half their net worth, nearly all of their labor and their most stressed paradox: that they were themselves English slaves.

So fiercely did white Virginians covet their liberty, so proud and powerful were they in disposing of their human property, that there seems to be no parallel for it anywhere, except perhaps in the time of Republican Rome, that golden idyll so beloved by classically-educated Virginia gentlemen. Of course, the slaves in this latter-day idyll do not have names. Literacy being power in Virginia, the mark of individual slaves on history is a frail "X." Their status as enduring metaphor is however unassailable.

One of America's best critics, Richard Poirier, has described the "extravagances of language" in American letters as "an exultation . . . of consciousness momentarily set free." "The most interesting American books," he wrote, "are an image of the creation of America itself, of the effort . . . to 'Build therefore your own world.'. . . They are bathed in the myths of American history; they carry the metaphoric burden of a great dream of freedom – of the expansion of national consciousness into the vast spaces of a continent and the absorption of those spaces into ourselves."[3] Poirier was talking about American prose fiction; in particular, 19th-Century American novels. Whether the writings of 18th-Century Virginians were bathed in the myths of history he did not say. But certainly it is hard to imagine a more compelling image of the creation of America itself than Thomas Jefferson's Declaration of Independence – or one more devoted to building its own world.

To emphatically declare the right to liberty a self-evident truth even as he was continuing to hold (in his own words) "the

[3] Richard Poirier, *A World Elsewhere* (Oxford and New York, 1966), pp. 7, 3;

[slavery] wolf by the ears" not only defied belief; it made a mockery of it.[4]

Yet Virginians did more than embrace the paradoxes of Jefferson's great dream, they added to them. Having blamed the British government for bringing slavery to America, they did not hesitate to blame themselves – with equal vehemence – for having failed to rise above their own "dissipative indolence."[5]

By the time this book opens, the Virginians had been in a bad mood for years. Most grew one cash crop, tobacco, commerce in which was exclusively limited to Great Britain. Barred by law from issuing their own currency and obliged to pay excessive prices for the latest fashions, they were incensed to find darned holes in their "new" stockings just arrived from London. They liked to say "an English pronunciation is best," but found English condescension intolerable. They hated "dependency"; but given the chance would gladly accept appointment to a crown office. Virginia society was not like that of the other colonies. It was more proud; it was also more English. Virginians were not like other Americans. They were "prodigious in spirit" – even the Bostonians said that.

"Prodigious in spirit", "the most spirited and consistent of any" – one delegate to the First Continental Congress called the Bostonians "mere milksops" compared to the Virginians.[6] First impressions are made to be changed of course and what was once said of all the delegates from Virginia, even the most conservative, would eventually be reserved for just one: Patrick

4   Thomas Jefferson, *Notes on the State of Virginia* (Charlottesville, 1783)

5   *The Diary of Colonel Landon Carter*, Jack P. Greene, ed. (2 vols., Richmond, 1987), 1: 512.

6   Quoted in George Morgan, *The True Patrick Henry* (J.B. Lippincott and Co., 1907); reprint, American Foundation Publications, Bridgewater, Va. 2000) p.157. The delegate was Joseph Reed.

Henry, Jr. That is too bad, not because Henry was any less prodigious than legend tells, but because what made him so was his unique ability to give voice to the prodigious spirit of America. Nor is it difficult to trace the origins of this spirit to the mental and physical landscape of Virginia: the widely-dispersed, largely self-sufficient farms and plantations, each of them a virtual "little city"; the sense of near total autonomy that left the Virginia planter free to perfect his tyranny over his slaves at the very moment he was reacting with indignation to British encroachments on his own liberty.[7]

Slavery made white planters rich; but it was a wealth counted in lives which could not be spent. Slavery degraded the slave; but like all absolute power it also weakened and corrupted the master, belying his affectations of moral superiority and defeating his attempts at economic independence. Slavery was evil; and slavery supplied the Virginians with a handy metaphor for British tyranny. In short, Virginia bequeathed America a definition of liberty as deeply conflicted as Virginia itself; one which was linked, both figuratively and in fact, to a despotism far worse than any practiced by Parliament.

A subtitle for this series might be "the untold story of an unknown revolution." But any reader expecting to encounter the usual stuff of which revolutions are made – war, political and social chaos, or a French-Revolution-style reign of terror – is in for a surprise. There was no British massacre in Williamsburg, accordingly, there was no cause for vengeance; no garrisoning of British troops in Virginia houses, and thus no reason to complain of oppression; no closing of Virginia's ports, and thus no need to punish an entire population for the acts of a few. Instead of a

[7] Letter of Phillip V. Fithian to John Peck, August 12, 1774, *Journal and Letters of Phillip Vickers Fithian*, ed. Hunter Dickinson Farish (Williamsburg, 1957), p. 161, 238fn1.

Battle of Lexington and Concord there was a *threatened* march on Williamsburg, not by a British occupation force, but a ragtag collection of militia commanded by Patrick Henry. The first conflict of the war in Virginia was no Bunker Hill, just a sad mowing-down of British grenadiers at Great Bridge, a miserable village defended by a wretched fort called "the Hogpen." Had not Cornwallis retired to Yorktown in 1781, Virginians might have been bystanders to their own revolution.

But if Virginia's battle against tyranny seems to lack for excitement, it is not because Virginians lacked for patriotic fury. It is because their battle, enacted as it was on the stage of a slave colony, seemed so preposterous. Instead of mob action on Boston Common we have Thomas Jefferson's lifelong effort to "carefully avoid . . . every possible act or manifestation on [the] . . . subject [of slavery.]"[8]

This a series about a revolution that was destined from the start to be imperfect; about a place and a people who have yet to find their rightful place in histories of the period. Not all of these people were rebels. Not all of their actions can be described as revolutionary. The Virginians liked to argue; they liked to write even more, and often kept copies of their letters. Some of their letters now seem artful, some merely oblique and some (like those of Patrick Henry) so effortlessly transparent as to require us to imagine an audience to make them intelligible. Their value lies less in what they say than in how they enact the stressed ironies of life in Virginia. Virginians really did see themselves as actors on a stage, but it was a classic, not a Georgian stage, and they were not only the principal actors but a chorus reflecting on the meaning of their actions. To treat the Virginians' well-chosen words merely as a quarry for facts would be silly. Virginians used words to aggrandize.

8   Thomas Jefferson to George Logan, 11 May 1805, Paul Leicester Ford, ed., *The Writings of Thomas Jefferson*, 10 vols. (New York, 1892–1899), 9: 141.

So what do Virginians' words tell us about them and their revolution? Among other things they tell us that for lack of good cause to rebel, Virginians seized upon a deeply unpopular royal governor, Lord Dunmore, and found in him a plausible caricature of everything they despised; that the prodigious spirit of the Virginians was both a reaction to and a predisposition for tyranny; and that if Williamsburg is the most studied 18th-Century city in the world, Virginia itself remains mostly unread.

It is not too late to put that to rights. The close reading of the letters and diaries of historical figures is not an arcane science, any more than say, the close reading of a novel. Nor must it lead to new approaches to Virginia itself, though it may challenge some old ones. This is not a history of Revolutionary Virginia, though it might qualify as a prospectus for one, being in part a meditation on a theme of neglect as revealed in the works of those historians who like to think of 18th-Century Virginia as a place far, far away; that is, anything but a slave colony. For some people, the discovery of Founder DNA in the descendants of slaves will always be a revelation.

The popularity of books like Joseph Ellis's *American Sphinx* suggests Americans are willing to reinvest in Virginia's Founders, even the fallen ones, as long as the story is well told. I hope so, as the story of Virginia and the Virginia Founders is the back story of America itself, a narrative less about a race of heroes than a few large souls laboring to transform irony into myth. My focus on those ironies should not be misunderstood. It is in fact a manifestation of my esteem. Like Gov. Francis Fauquier, who once incautiously told their lordships at the Ministry that he had "come to love these Virginians," I have found what I abhor inextricably entwined with what I most admire.

GEORGE MORROW

Acknowledgements

Dr. Samuel Johnson once said, "It is wonderful how a man will sometimes turn over half a library to make just one book." After ten years of nearly constant work on this series, I find that I have not only turned over half a library, but a good part of my life. New friends have become old ones. Some very good friends who read the essays in this series in their very earliest versions are now gone. Meanwhile, the library – I am speaking of the ever-expanding library of the internet – has only gotten larger.

It is impossible to name everyone who helped make this series, but some I must mention. There would be no series without the love, encouragement and help of my wife, Joan Morrow. But for the welcoming attitude, expert assistance and criticism of two truly fine historians of the period, Rhys Isaac and James Horn, I would still be trying to distinguish the forest from the trees. The encouragement I received from my two chief non professional readers, Joan and Terry Thomas, turned a mere collection of dates, people and events into a study of the character of Williamsburg. Other people who read one or more of the essays and made helpful comments include my 90-year-old aunt Rosemary Bauder, Paul and Joan Wernick, Richard Schumann, Michael Fincham, Ken and Judith Simmons, Fred Fey, Cary Carson, Jon Kite and Al Louer. I also wish in particular to thank Jon Kite for obtaining the French army dossier of John Skey Eustace and for translating one of Jack Eustace's overwrought pamphlets from the French. Richard Schumann ,

James Horn and Roger Hudson kindly consented to do prefaces for one of the booklets in this series. Al Louer and Paul Freiling of Colonial Williamsburg arranged for me to see Williamsburg from the roof of the Governor's Palace, a view that put time itself in perspective .

Those who are subscribers to the British quarterly, *Slightly Foxed*, described on its website as "The Real Reader's Quarterly," will recognize some similarities between the booklets in this series and that magazine. The resemblance is no accident. When I saw *Slightly Foxed* for the first time, I immediately realized that it was the perfect model, in size, material and design for what I was looking for. With that in mind, I contacted Andrew Evans at 875 Design, the English book design firm responsible for its appearance, and asked him if would be willing to take on this project. He said, "yes," and it was not long before he and I had assembled a team of people who not only seemed to know what I wanted but were able to give me something I never expected to find: new ideas on the subject matter. I especially want to thank Gail Pirkis, the publisher of *Slightly Foxed*, for recommending Roger Hudson as editor for this series. Roger is not only a highly accomplished writer in his own right, he is truly a writer's editor.

Sadly, the genial spirit who presided over the series, read and commented on virtually every booklet and guided me through its development, died while the series was still in production. I am speaking of Rhys Isaac, the Pulitzer Prize-winning author of what is still the best book ever written on late colonial Virginia, *The Transformation of Virginia*. Rhys' presence at our dinner table will be deeply missed. But he will also be missed from the profession of history, where his exuberant writing style and elegiac approach to the past daily gave the lie to the sour souls who think history is about settling scores.

As I began these Acknowledgments with a quotation from

Samuel Johnson I would like to end with one *about* Johnson. It was spoken by someone who did not know him well, but knew of him very well, William Gerard Hamilton. For me, it is Rhys Isaac's epitaph: " He has made a chasm, which not only nothing can fill up, but which nothing has a tendency to fill up. – Johnson is dead. – Let us go to the next best; – There is no nobody; – no man can be said to put you in mind of Johnson."

About the Author

GEORGE MORROW brings a lifetime of experience to bear on the characters of the people featured in this series. He has been a university instructor, lawyer, general counsel for a *Fortune* 100 company, the CEO of two major health care organizations and a management consultant. He received his academic training in textual analysis and literary theory from Rutgers and Brown Universities. He lives in Williamsburg with his wife, Joan, and two in-your-face Siamese cats, Pete and Pris.

WILLIAMSBURG IN CHARACTER

> "Tribal, atavistic forces were abroad,
> both in England and in the
> Thirteen Colonies, and in them
> the Enlightenment met its match."

From the Preface by Roger Hudson

Francis Fauquier   Norborne Berkeley,
                          Lord Botetourt

The Day They Buried Great Britain

Williamsburg in Character No. 3

Coming December 2010

WILLIAMSBURG IN CHARACTER

To be published soon

The Day They Buried Great Britain

His funeral was perhaps the grandest – and saddest – ever held in Williamsburg. At one o'clock on Friday afternoon, October 19, 1770 all the bells in Williamsburg began to toll. Precisely at two, those who had received an invitation to follow Botetourt's corpse to its place of interment in the chapel of the College of William and Mary gathered at the Governor's Palace. At three o'clock, the coffin was placed on the hearse and the cortege, passing through a corridor of militia, moved down Palace Street to Bruton Parish church for the reading of the funeral service.

It was all done with strict attention to rank and decorum as befit the man and the sadness of the day. If the notice in the *Gazette* sounded epochal it was because solemn words and high ritual were part of the event, but it is also true that the event was felt by many Virginians, even then, to mark the passing of an age:

THE HEARSE

Preceded by two mutes, and three on each side the hearse,
Outward of whom walked the pall bearers,
Composed of six of his Majesty's Council,
And the Hon. the Speaker, and Richard Bland, Esq;
of the House of Burgesses.
His Excellency's servants, in deep mourning.
The Gentlemen of the Clergy, and
Professors of the College.

Clerk of the Church, and Organist.
Immediately followed the hearse the Chief Mourners
Gentlemen of the Faculty.
Mayor, Recorder, Aldermen, and
Common Council of the city,
With the mace born before them.
Gentlemen of the Law, and Clerk of the General Court,
Ushers, Students, and Scholars of
William and Mary college,
All having white hatbands and gloves,
And then the company, which was very numerous,
Two and two.

When the procession reached the church's west entrance, the coffin was removed from the hearse. An honor guard of gentlemen carried it to the center of the church and placed it on a black carpet. The attendees took their seats, each according to rank. The vicar, Rev. Mr. Woolls, led them in an anthem with Peter Pelham, Bruton Parish's organist (and Botetourt's part-time clerk), at the organ. The Commissary, Mr. Horrocks, delivered the sermon. It was from Psalm XLII, *Put thy trust in God*, which, "joined to the deep affliction felt by the whole audience," drew tears from many. The coffin, said to be made "of lead with a cover of crimson velvet adorned with silver handles," was then replaced on the hearse and taken to William and Mary for burial under Botetourt's favorite pew.

On October 30, William Nelson wrote to the Duke of Beaufort, informing him of the sad fact of his uncle's death, the grandeur of his funeral ("attended with some expence") and the colony's intentions with respect to assembling and disposing of Botetourt's Virginia estate. The letter, with its attached inventory of Botetourt's effects, reached Badminton on New Year's Day. The Duke replied at once, complimenting Nelson for "directing so very handsome a funeral and conducting it with so much Order and Decency." He also offered to pay any expence incurred. Nelson's proposal for the disposition of Lord Botetourt's things was also acceptable to the Duke. He asked only that he be permitted to erect a monument to his "dear uncle" in the college chapel. As for Botetourt's state coach and the paintings of the King and Queen, brought with him to Virginia, the Duke hoped that the colony would accept them as "a small return . . . for the many . . . marks of . . . esteem they shew'd" when Botetourt was ill, and for the "Regard . . . paid to his Memory, in his funeral."

The Duke's request that he might be allowed to erect a monument to Botetourt was laid before the Virginia General Assembly by William Nelson at its July 1771 session. The burgesses liked the idea; liked it so well that they voted to fund a statue at public expense. "We should . . . think ourselves wanting in . . . Regard . . . to our Country," they declared, "did we not seize this first Opportunity of publicly paying a just tribute to so high a character." Nelson was told to procure "an elegant Statue of his late Excellency . . . in Marble . . . with proper inscriptions."

The statue, by English sculptor Richard Hayward, arrived in Virginia in mid-1773. It cost nearly £1,000, an extraordinarily large sum for a colony still teetering on the edge of bankruptcy.

Col. Richard Bland, whose 1765 essay attacking the constitutionality of the Stamp Act would later be viewed as the first literary shot of the rebellion, composed the inscription on Botetourt's statue.

He praised the late Governor as someone who had sought to heal Virginia's wounds:

"AMERICA, BEHOLD YOUR FRIEND WHO LEAVING HIS NATIVE COUNTRY DECLINED THOSE ADDITIONAL HONOURS WHICH WERE THERE IN STORE FOR HIM THAT HE MIGHT HEAL YOUR WOUNDS

AND RESTORE TRANQUILITY AND HAPPINESS TO THIS EXTENSIVE
CONTINENT; WITH WHAT ZEAL AND ANXIETY HE PURSUED THESE
GLORIOUS OBJECTS, VIRGINIA, THUS BEARS HER GRATEFULL
TESTAMONY" (Capitals in original).

It was a fine tribute – but perhaps not as fine as that of the
many American soldiers who came upon Botetourt's statue
during the war, read the inscription, and chose to leave it
unharmed.

Col. Bland's was the official, governmental response to the
passing of Lord Botetourt. It was left to Northern Neck planter
Landon Carter, writing in his journal on October 15, 1768, to
appropriate his soul for Virginia:

> Yesterday came a letter endorsed from Colo. Tayloe with
> the death of Ld. Botetourt, our Governour, who left us
> the 13th in the morning. A melancholly piece of news. A
> fine Gentleman is dead and truly Noble in his Public
> character. He, as anecdote says, was pitch'd upon to be
> the Agent of a dirty tyrannic Ministry; but his virtues
> resisted such an employment and he became the instru-
> ment of a dawning happiness; and had he lived we should
> have been so: for through his active and exemplary virtue,
> order everywhere revived out of that confusion that our
> own dissipative indolence had thrown us into.

It was perhaps as close as anyone was to come to describing
Botetourt's greatness as a governor. Here on the one hand was
a great lord – and governor – who mixed good judgment with
affability. Here on the other was a gifted manager of people
who sensed Virginians' need for order and moral certainty and
supplied it.